NICK

SpongeBob SquarePants™

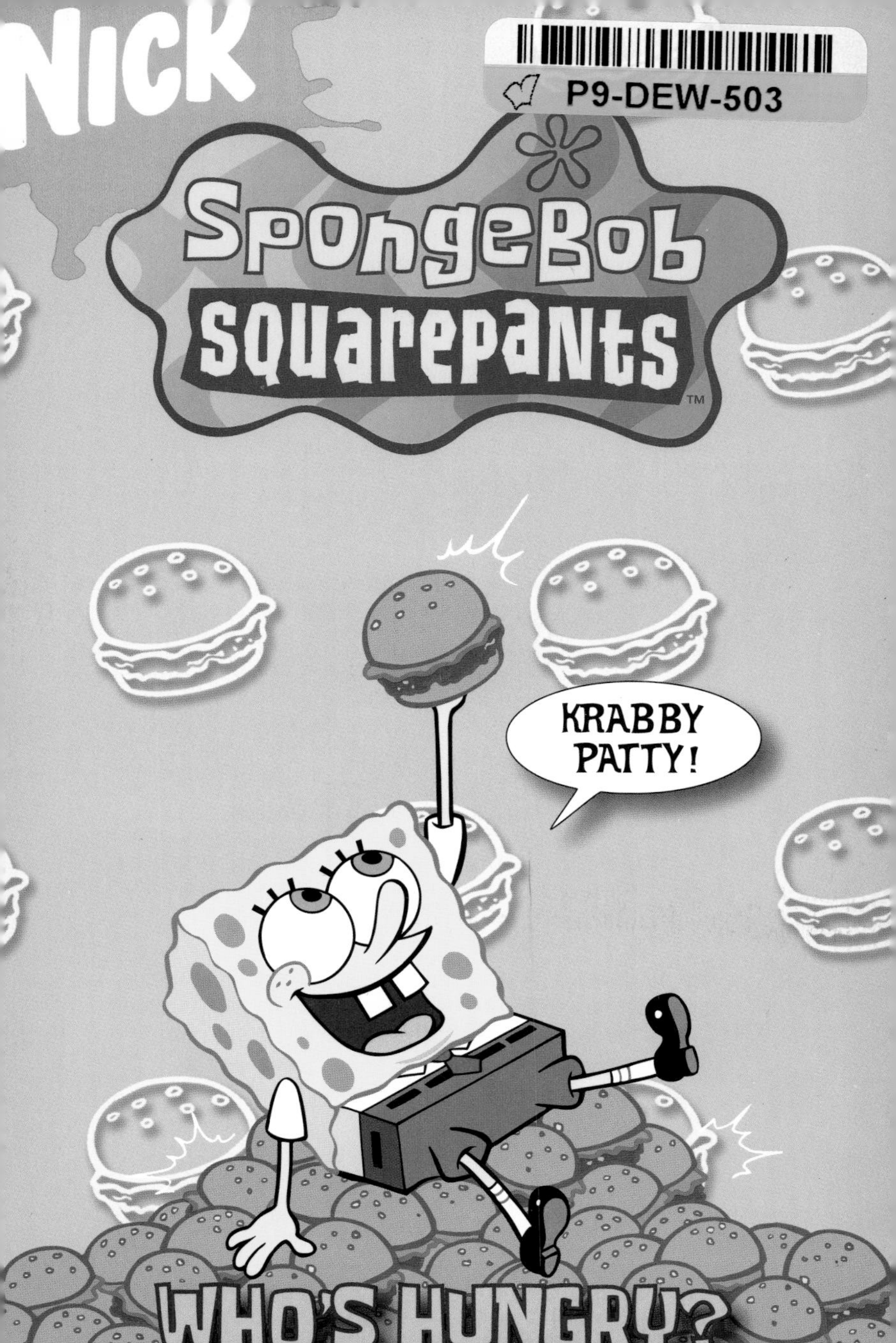
KRABBY PATTY!

WHO'S HUNGRY?

Editor - Zachary Rau
Contributing Editors - Steven Starkweather and Ian Mayer
Graphic Designer and Letterer - Peter Sattler
Cover Designer - Louis Csontos
Graphic Artist - Tomás Montalvo-Lagos and John Lo

Digital Imaging Manager - Chris Buford
Production Managers - Jennifer Miller and Mutsumi Miyazaki
Senior Designer - Anna Kernbaum
Senior Editor - Elizabeth Hurchalla
Managing Editor - Lindsey Johnston
VP of Production - Ron Klamert
Publisher & Editor in Chief - Mike Kiley
President & C.O.O. - John Parker
C.E.O. - Stuart Levy

E-mail: info@TOKYOPOP.com
Come visit us online at www.TOKYOPOP.com

A 🌐 **TOKYOPOP**® Cine-Manga® Book
TOKYOPOP Inc.
5900 Wilshire Blvd., Suite 2000
Los Angeles, CA 90036

SpongeBob Squarepants: Who's Hungry?

ISBN: 1-59816-919-X

First TOKYOPOP® printing: May 2006

10 9 8 7 6 5 4 3 2 1

Printed in the USA

NICK

SpongeBob SquarePants™

Created by Stephen Hillenburg

WHO'S HUNGRY?

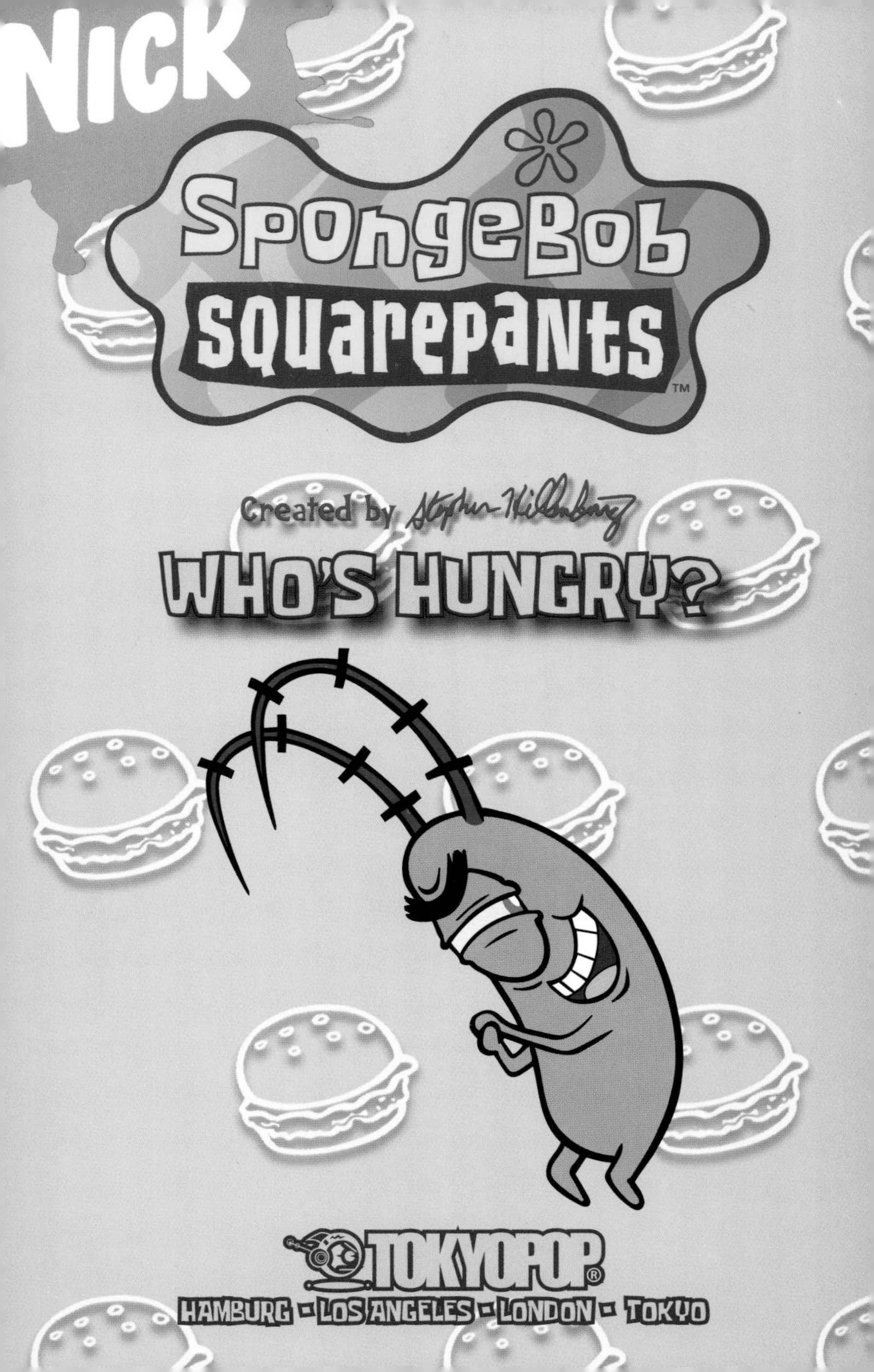

TOKYOPOP®

HAMBURG • LOS ANGELES • LONDON • TOKYO

NICK

SpongeBob SquarePants
™

SPONGEBOB SQUAREPANTS: An optimistic and friendly sea sponge who lives in a pineapple with his snail, Gary, and works as a fry cook at The Krusty Krab. He loves his job and is always looking on the bright side of everything.

PATRICK STAR: A starfish who is SpongeBob's best friend and neighbor.

GARY: Spongebob's pet snail. Meows like a cat.

PLANKTON: The owner of the Chum Bucket. Plankton's always plotting to steal Mr. Krab's Secret Krabby Patty recipe.

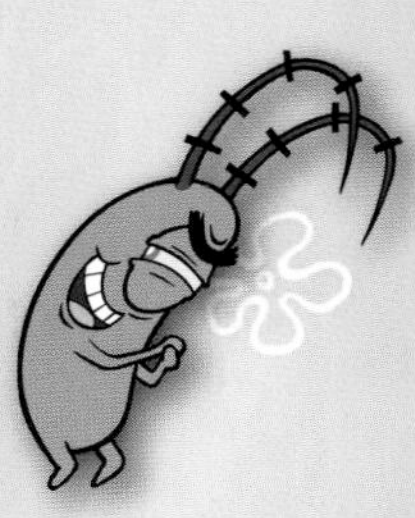

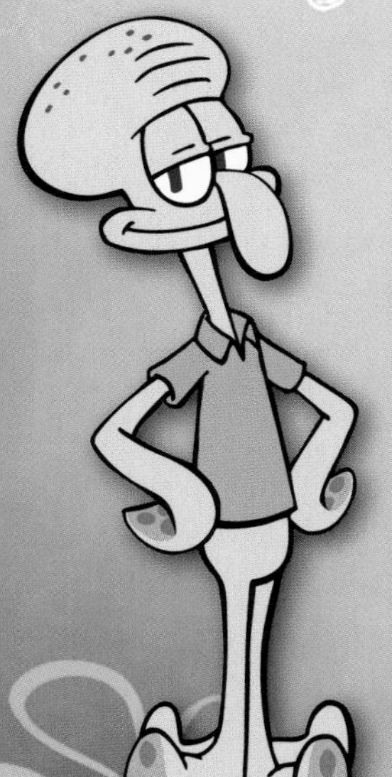

SQUIDWARD TENTACLES: A six-tentacled octopus who works as the cashier at The Krusty Krab. Unlike SpongeBob, Squidward tends to be negative about everything.

MR. KRABS: A crab who owns and runs The Krusty Krab. Mr. Krabs loves money and will do anything to avoid losing it.

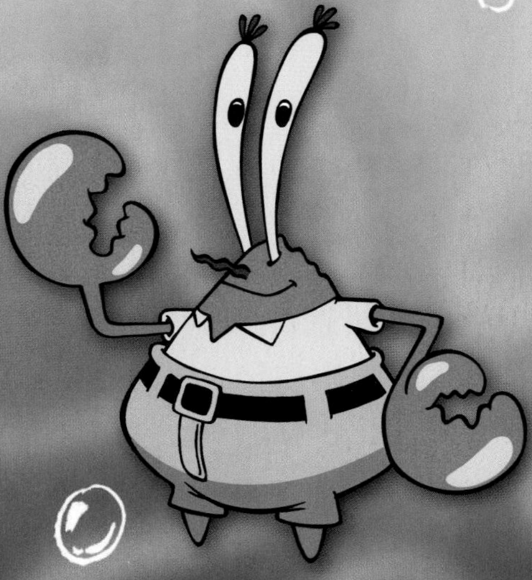

SpongeBob SquarePants™

WHO'S HUNGRY?

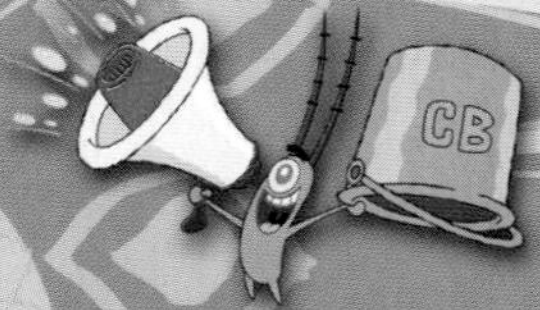

CB

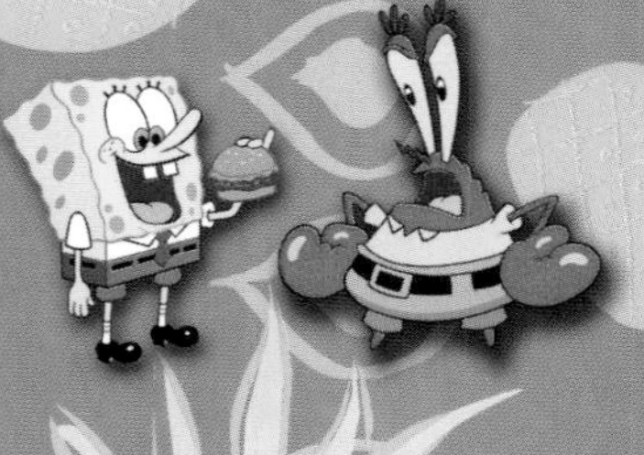

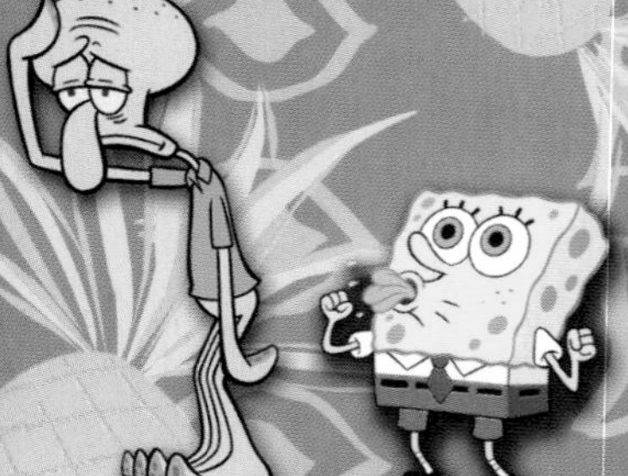

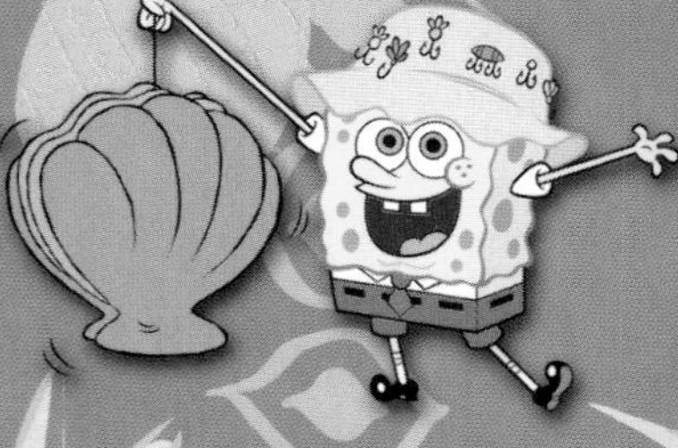

SpongeBob SquarePants

Welcome to the Chum Bucket

By Walt Dohrn, Paul Tibbett and Mr. Lawrence

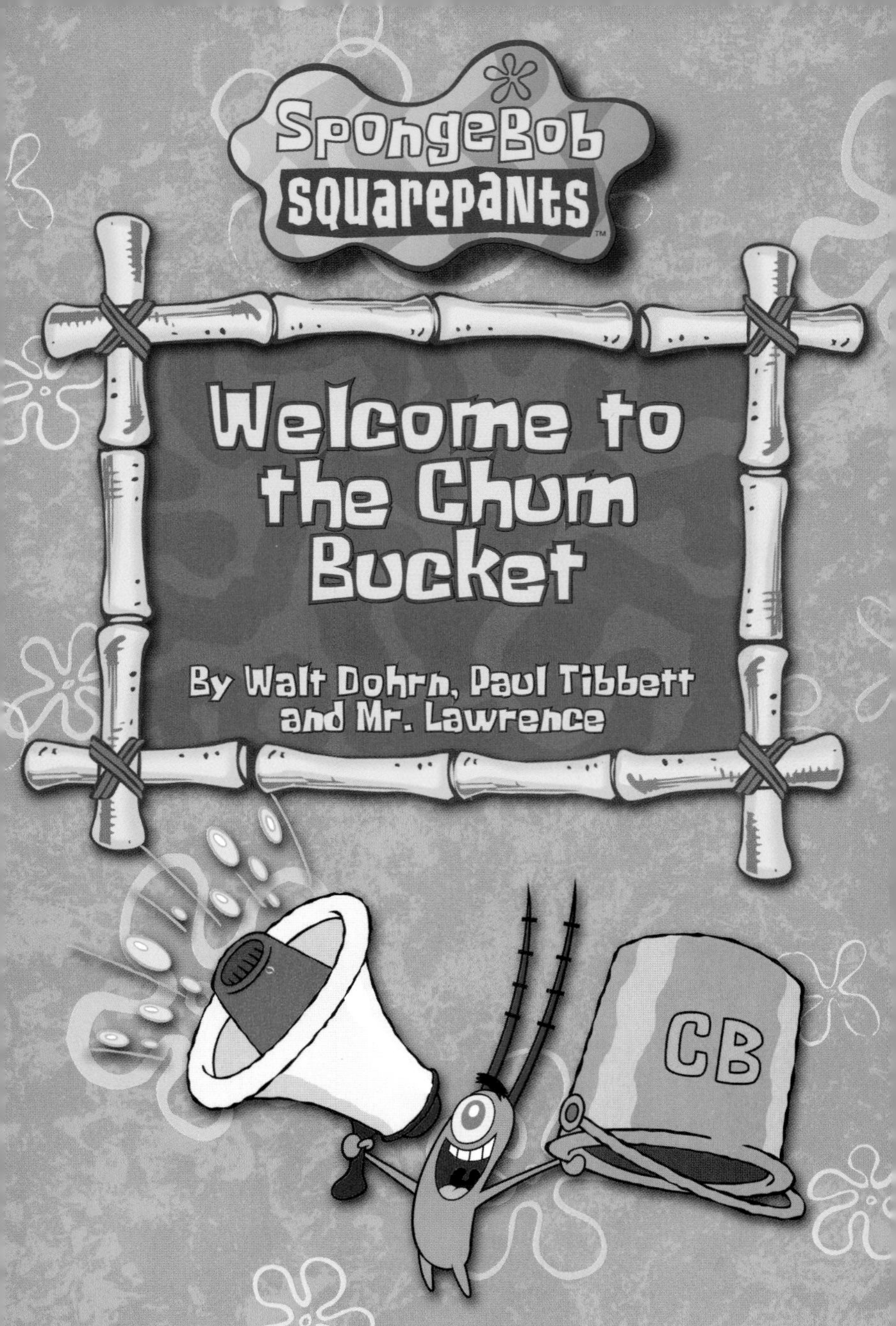
CB

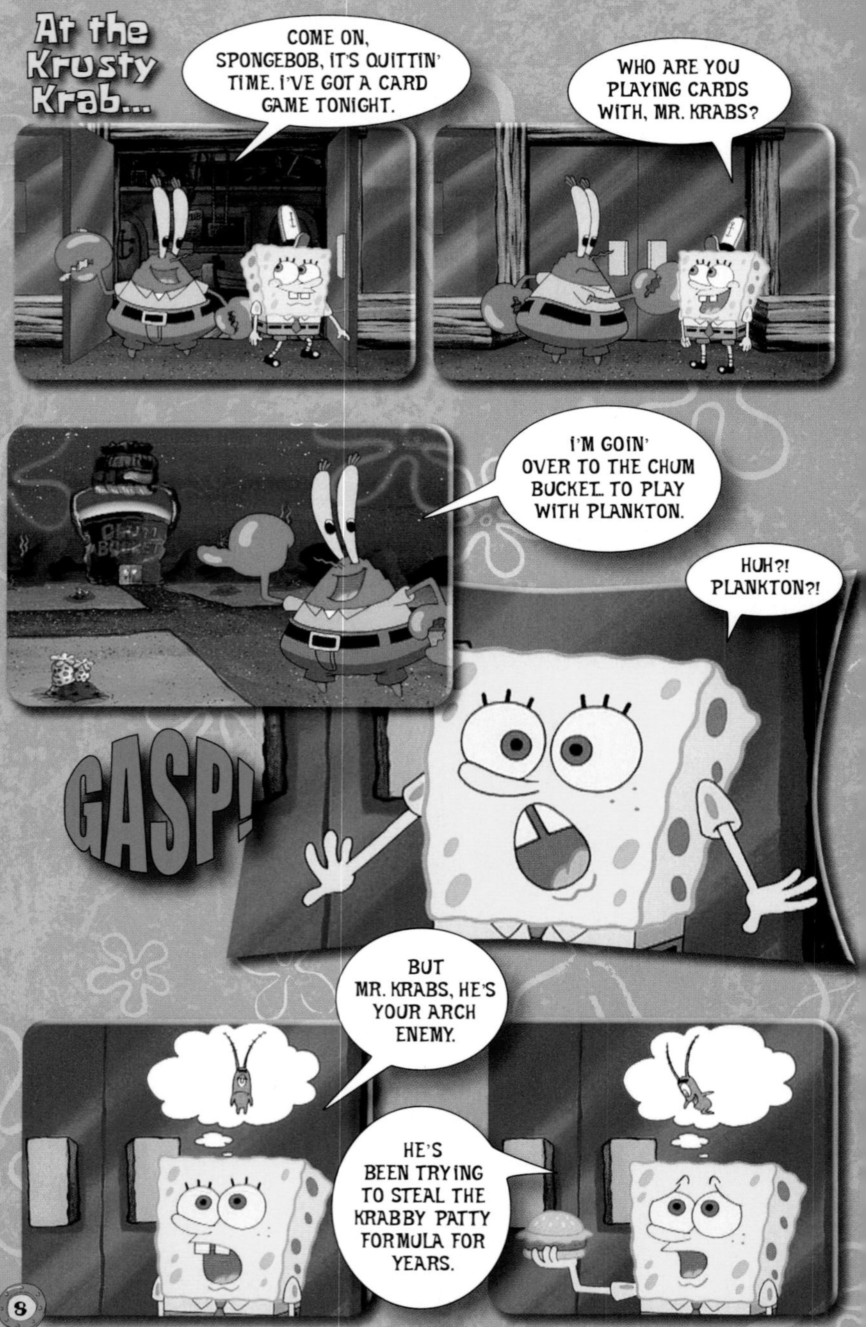
At the Krusty Krab...
COME ON, SPONGEBOB, IT'S QUITTIN' TIME. I'VE GOT A CARD GAME TONIGHT.
WHO ARE YOU PLAYING CARDS WITH, MR. KRABS?
I'M GOIN' OVER TO THE CHUM BUCKET... TO PLAY WITH PLANKTON.
HUH?! PLANKTON?!
GASP!
BUT MR. KRABS, HE'S YOUR ARCH ENEMY.
HE'S BEEN TRYING TO STEAL THE KRABBY PATTY FORMULA FOR YEARS.

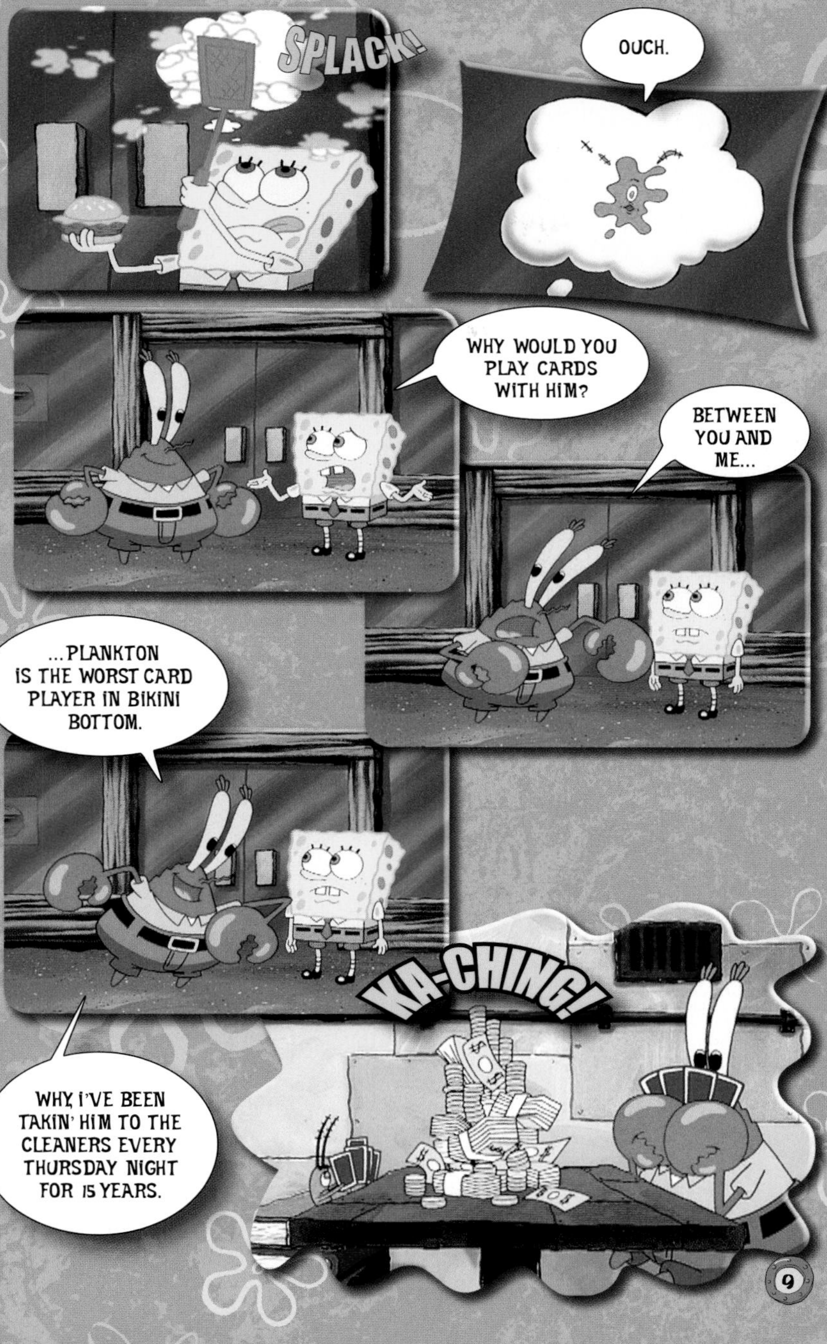
SPLACK!
OUCH.
WHY WOULD YOU PLAY CARDS WITH HIM?
BETWEEN YOU AND ME...
...PLANKTON IS THE WORST CARD PLAYER IN BIKINI BOTTOM.
WHY, I'VE BEEN TAKIN' HIM TO THE CLEANERS EVERY THURSDAY NIGHT FOR 15 YEARS.
KA-CHING!

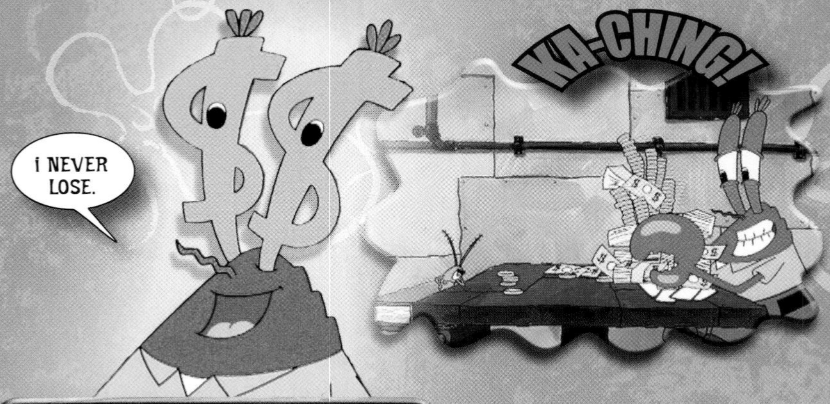
I NEVER LOSE.
KA-CHING!

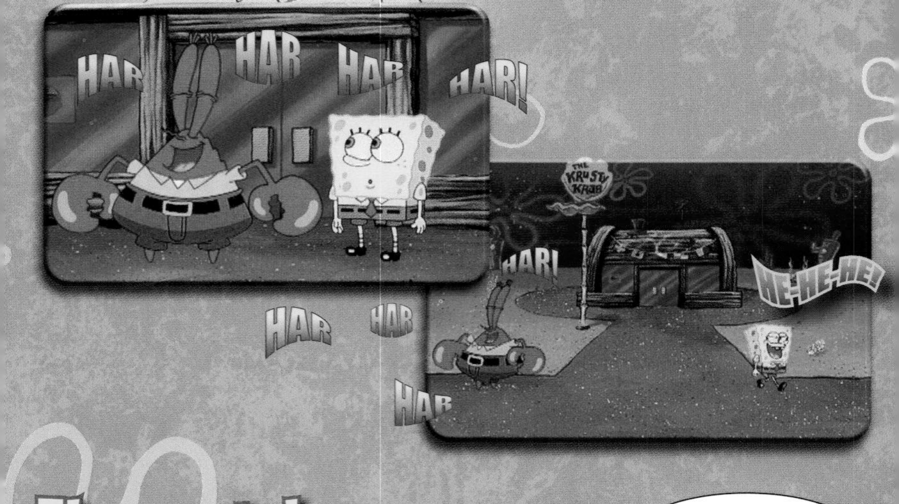
HAR
HAR
HAR
HAR!
HAR!
HAR
HAR
HAR
HE-HE-HE!

The next day...

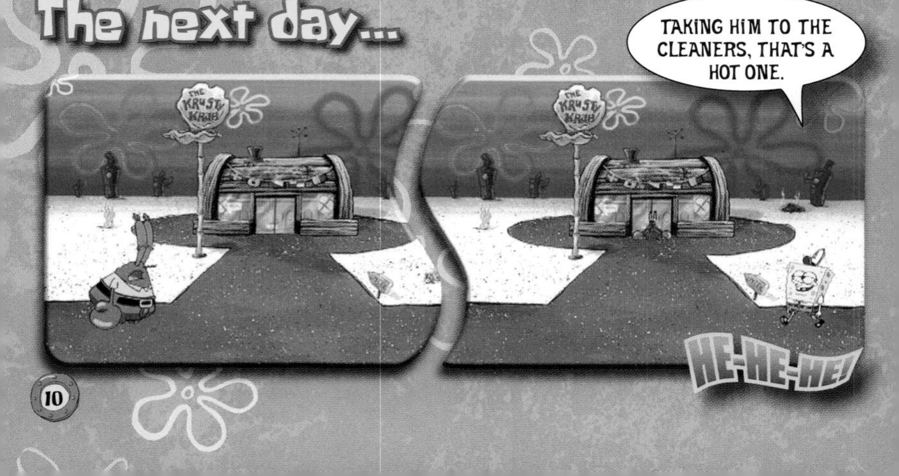
TAKING HIM TO THE CLEANERS, THAT'S A HOT ONE.
HE-HE-HE!

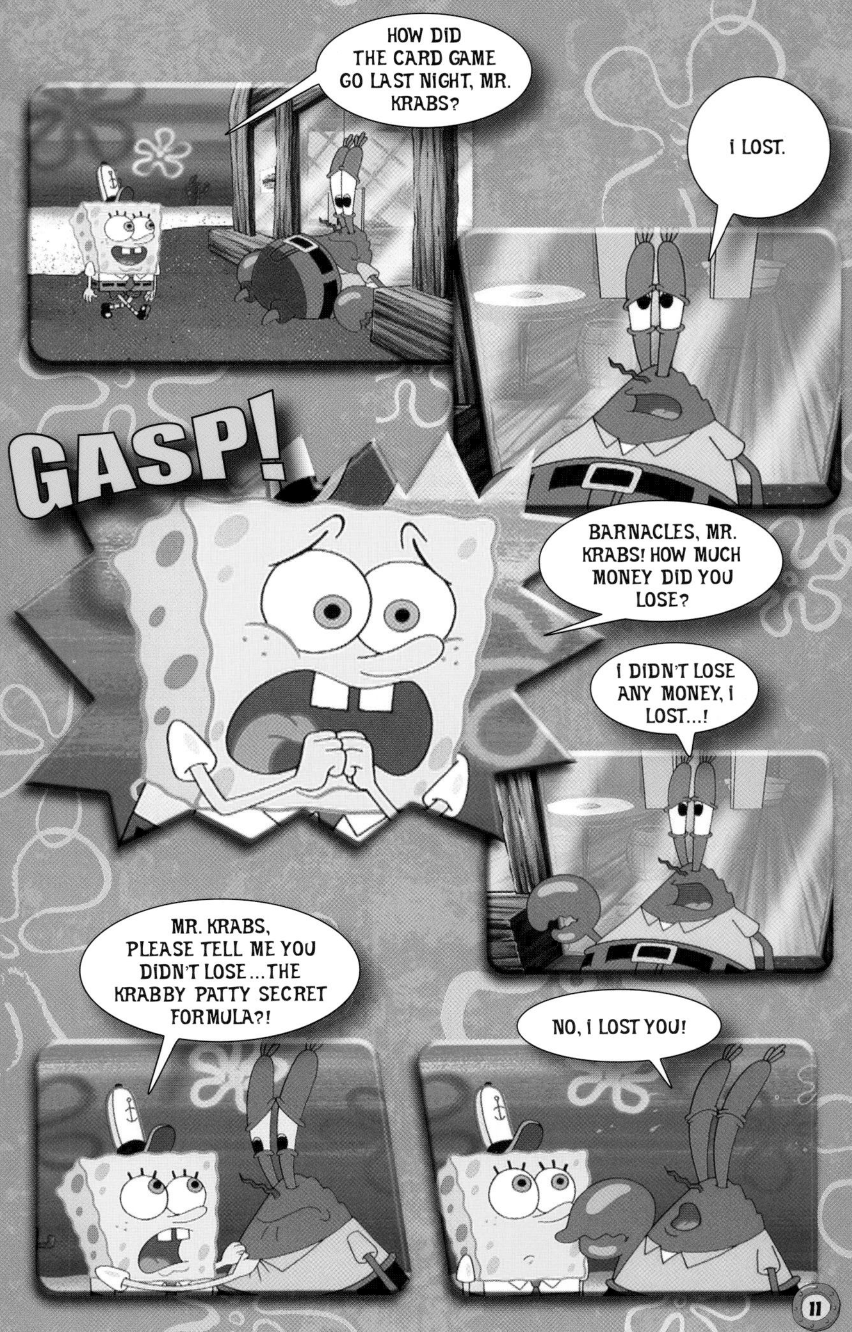
HOW DID THE CARD GAME GO LAST NIGHT, MR. KRABS?
I LOST.
GASP!
BARNACLES, MR. KRABS! HOW MUCH MONEY DID YOU LOSE?
I DIDN'T LOSE ANY MONEY, I LOST...!
MR. KRABS, PLEASE TELL ME YOU DIDN'T LOSE...THE KRABBY PATTY SECRET FORMULA?!
NO, I LOST YOU!

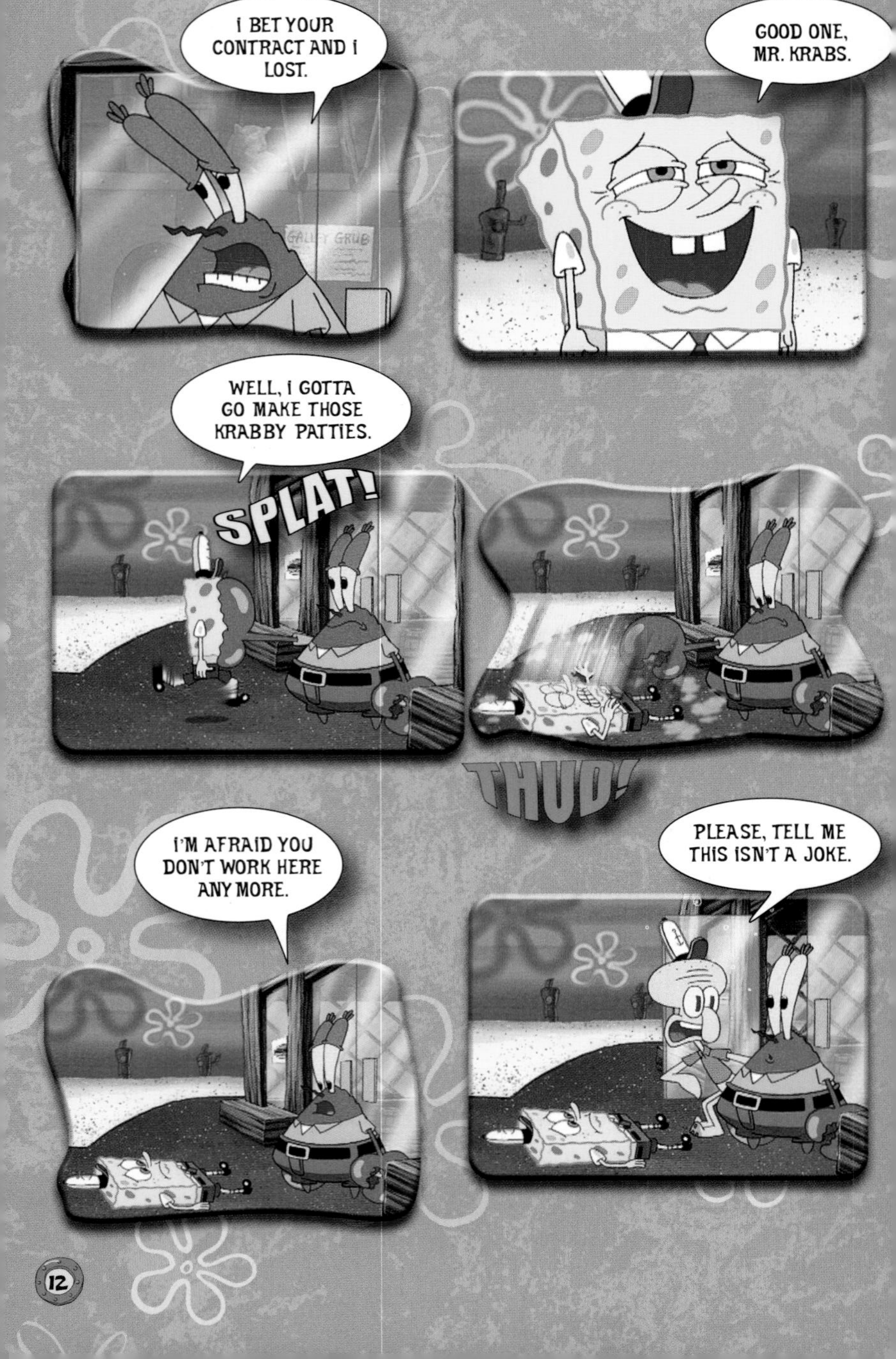
I BET YOUR CONTRACT AND I LOST.
GOOD ONE, MR. KRABS.
WELL, I GOTTA GO MAKE THOSE KRABBY PATTIES.
SPLAT!
THUD!
I'M AFRAID YOU DON'T WORK HERE ANY MORE.
PLEASE, TELL ME THIS ISN'T A JOKE.

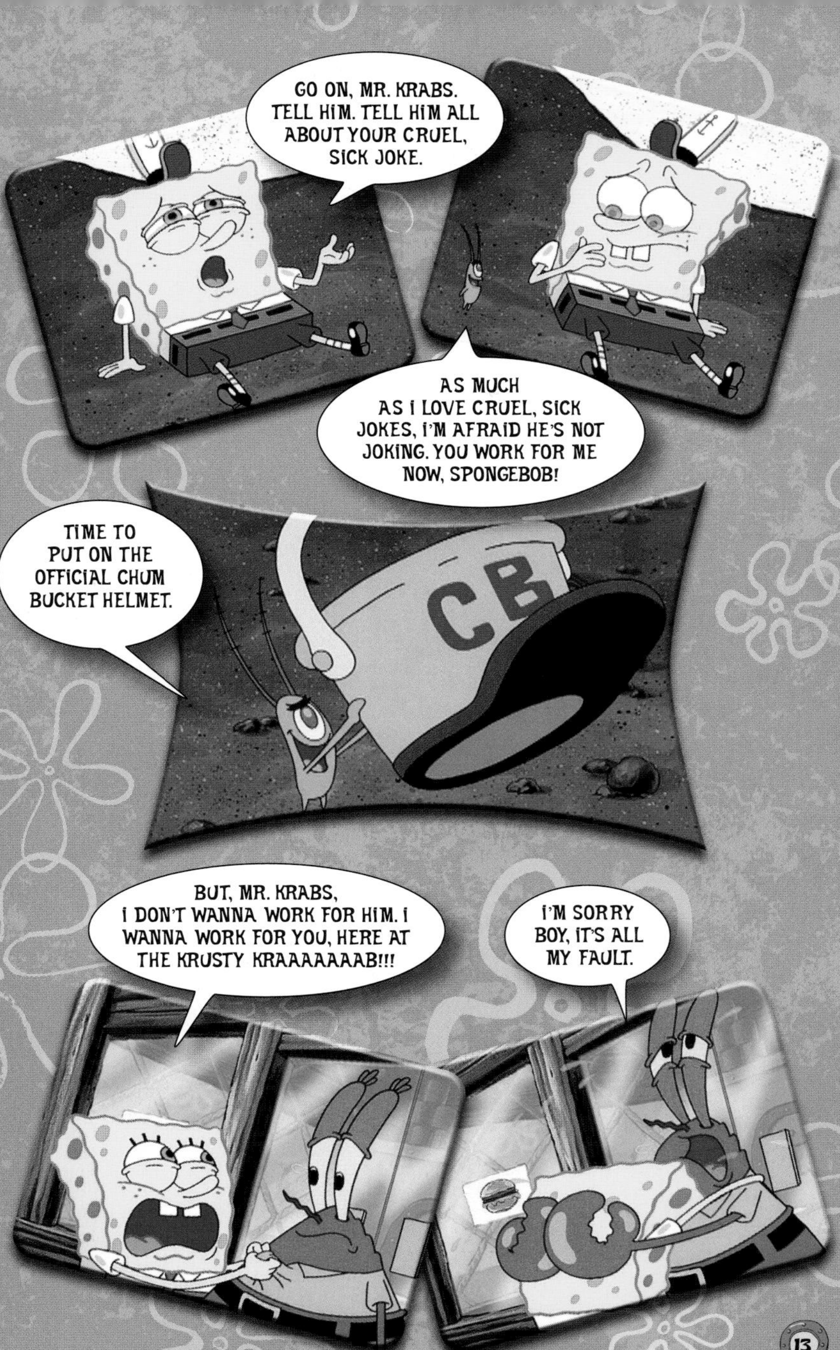
GO ON, MR. KRABS. TELL HIM. TELL HIM ALL ABOUT YOUR CRUEL, SICK JOKE.
AS MUCH AS I LOVE CRUEL, SICK JOKES, I'M AFRAID HE'S NOT JOKING. YOU WORK FOR ME NOW, SPONGEBOB!
TIME TO PUT ON THE OFFICIAL CHUM BUCKET HELMET.
CB
BUT, MR. KRABS, I DON'T WANNA WORK FOR HIM. I WANNA WORK FOR YOU, HERE AT THE KRUSTY KRAAAAAAAB!!!
I'M SORRY BOY, IT'S ALL MY FAULT.

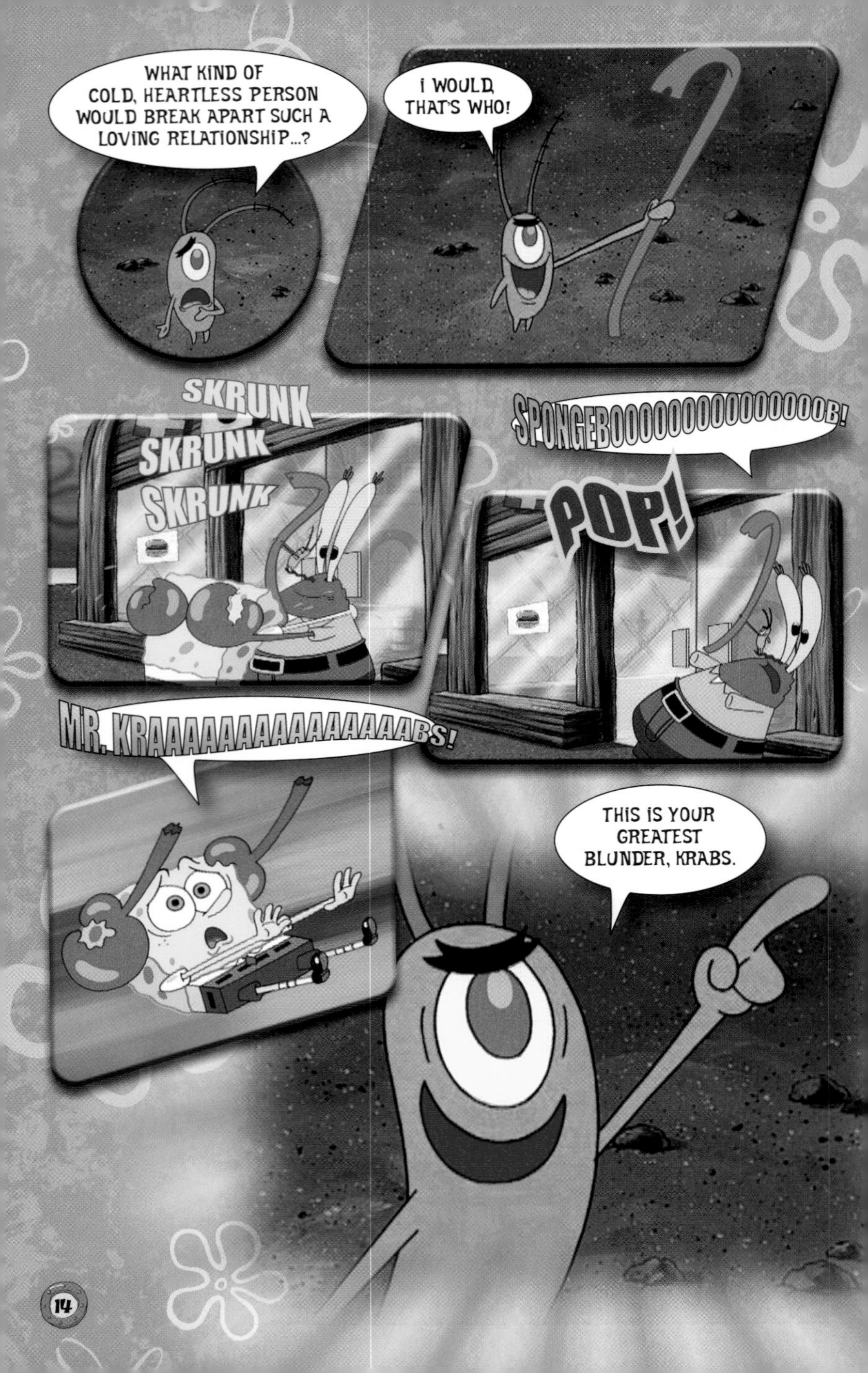
WHAT KIND OF COLD, HEARTLESS PERSON WOULD BREAK APART SUCH A LOVING RELATIONSHIP...?
I WOULD, THAT'S WHO!
SKRUNK
SKRUNK
SKRUNK
SPONGEBOOOOOOOOOOOOOOOB!
POP!
MR. KRAAAAAAAAAAAAAAABS!
THIS IS YOUR GREATEST BLUNDER, KRABS.

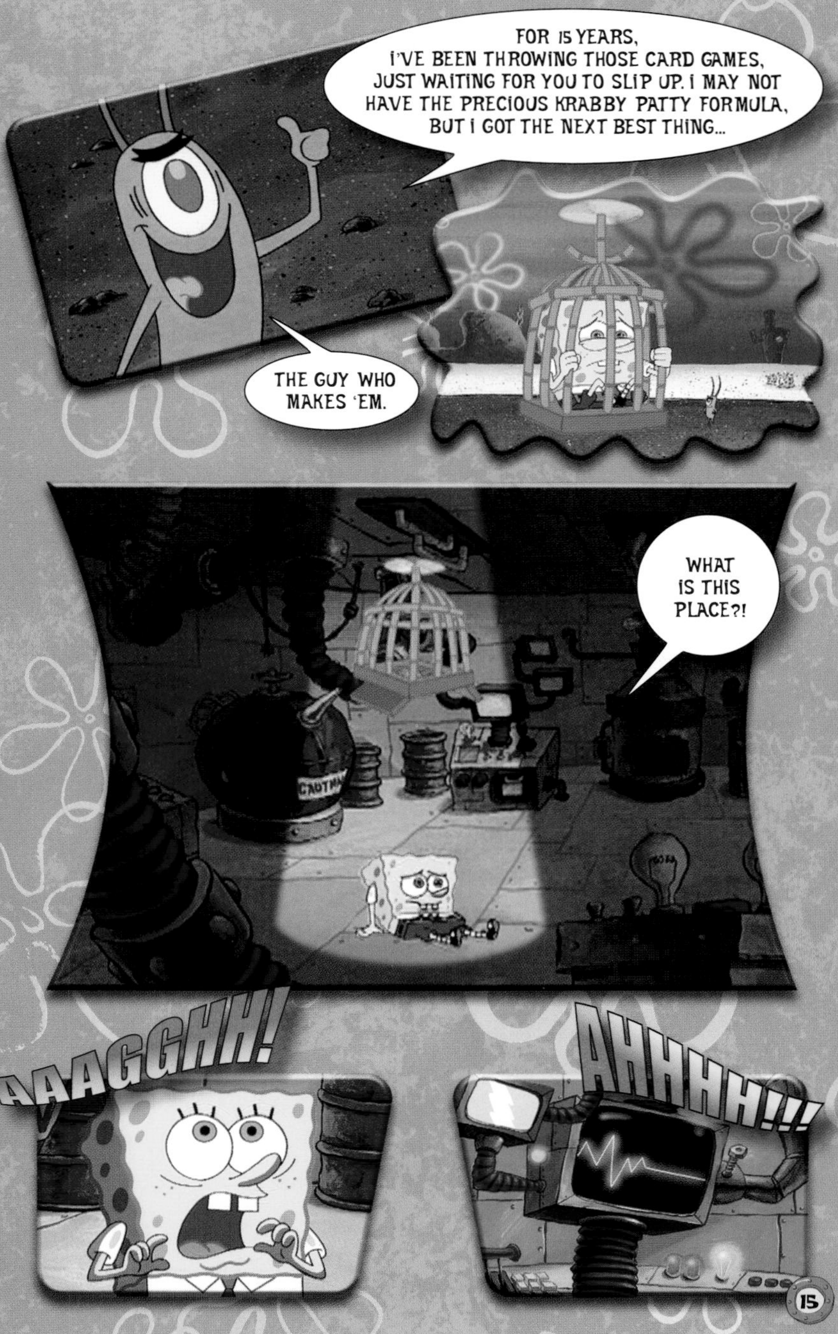
FOR 15 YEARS, I'VE BEEN THROWING THOSE CARD GAMES, JUST WAITING FOR YOU TO SLIP UP. I MAY NOT HAVE THE PRECIOUS KRABBY PATTY FORMULA, BUT I GOT THE NEXT BEST THING...
THE GUY WHO MAKES 'EM.
WHAT IS THIS PLACE?!
AAAGGHH!
AHHHHH!!!

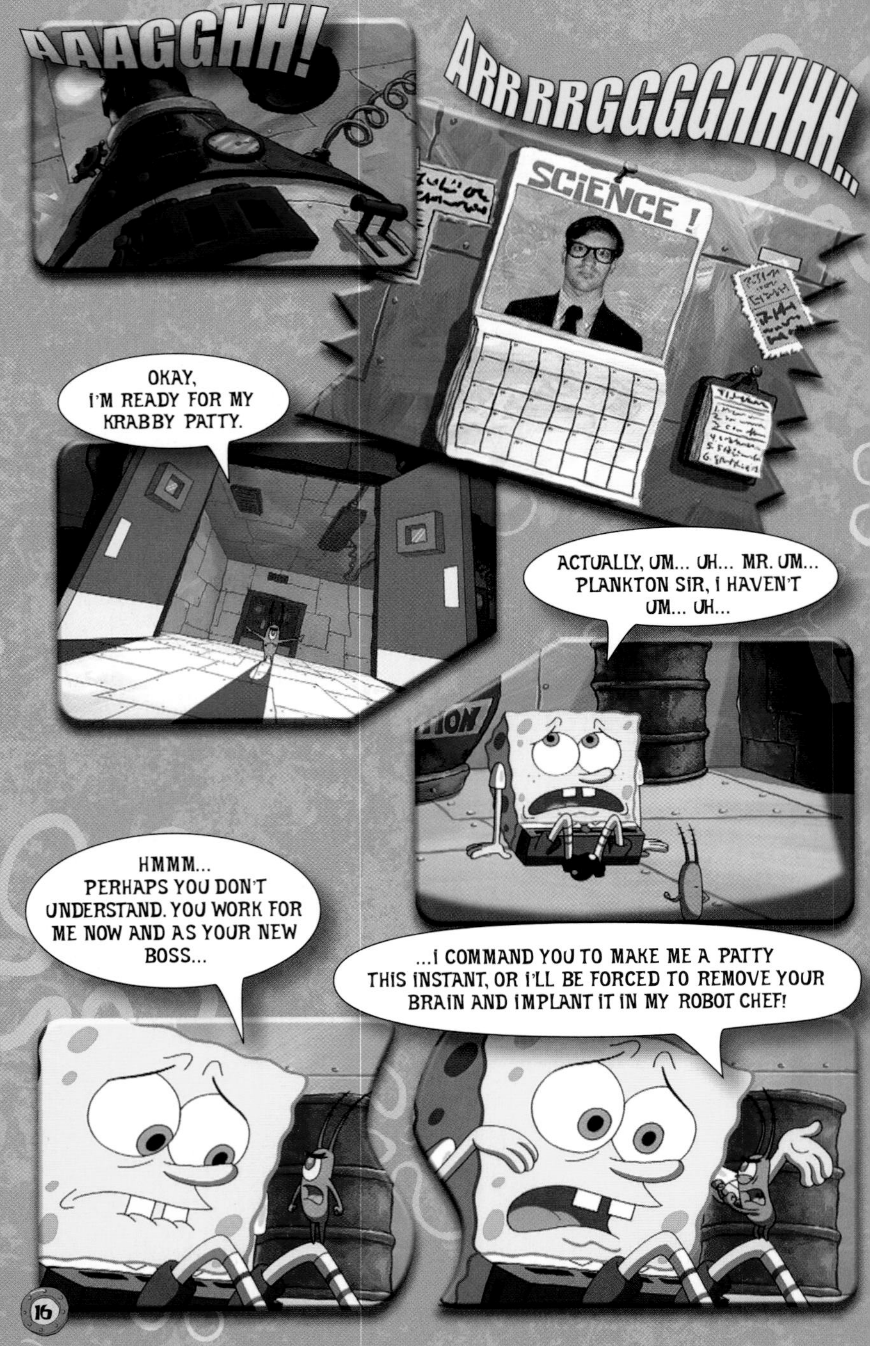
AAAGGHH!
ARRRRGGGGHHHH...
SCIENCE!
OKAY, I'M READY FOR MY KRABBY PATTY.
ACTUALLY, UM... UH... MR. UM... PLANKTON SIR, I HAVEN'T UM... UH...
HMMM... PERHAPS YOU DON'T UNDERSTAND. YOU WORK FOR ME NOW AND AS YOUR NEW BOSS...
...I COMMAND YOU TO MAKE ME A PATTY THIS INSTANT, OR I'LL BE FORCED TO REMOVE YOUR BRAIN AND IMPLANT IT IN MY ROBOT CHEF!

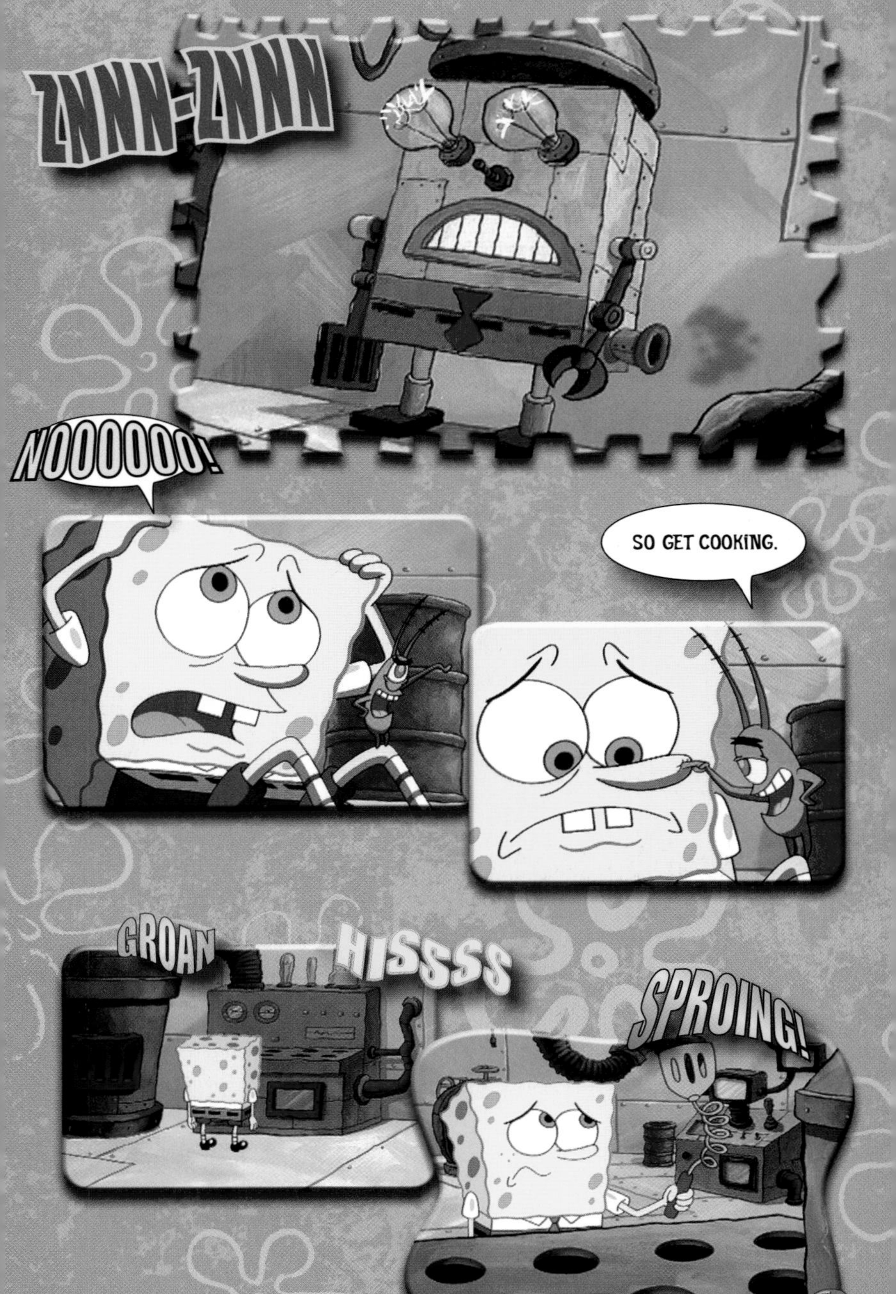
ZNNN-ZNNN
NOOOOOO!
SO GET COOKiNG.
GROAN
HISSSS
SPROING!

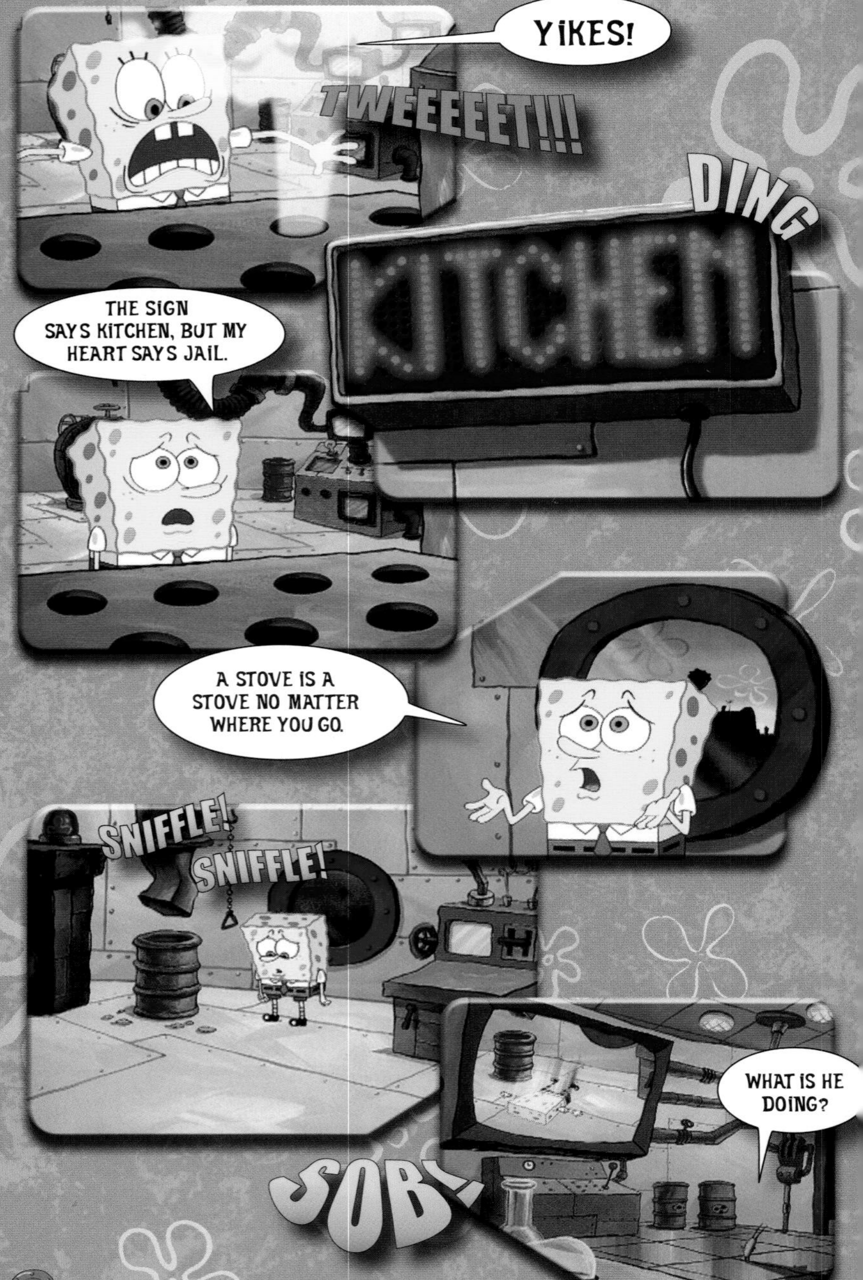
YIKES!
TWEEEEET!!!
DING
KITCHEN
THE SIGN SAYS KITCHEN, BUT MY HEART SAYS JAIL.
A STOVE IS A STOVE NO MATTER WHERE YOU GO.
SNIFFLE!
SNIFFLE!
SOB!
WHAT IS HE DOING?

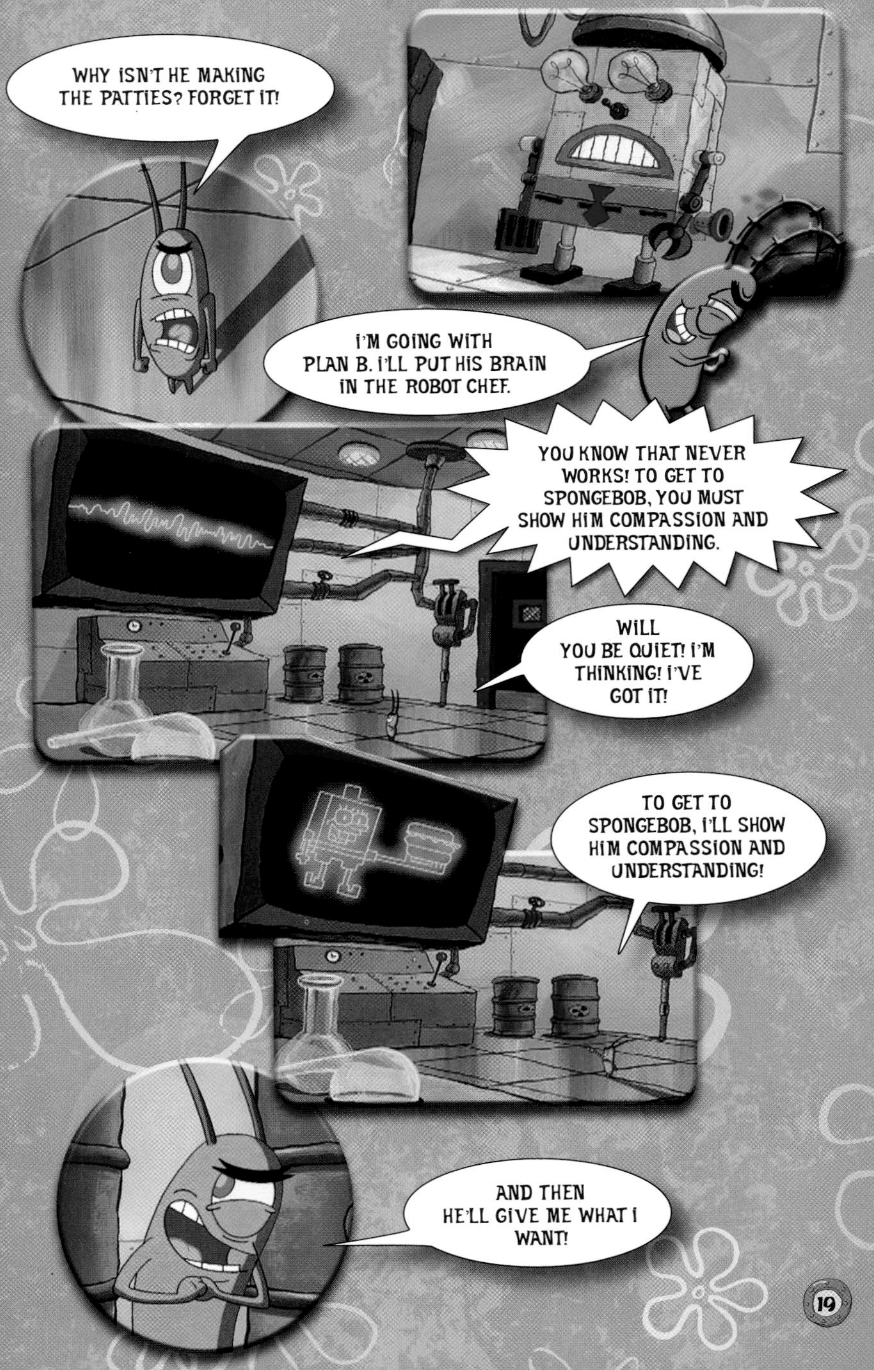
WHY ISN'T HE MAKING THE PATTIES? FORGET IT!
I'M GOING WITH PLAN B. I'LL PUT HIS BRAIN IN THE ROBOT CHEF.
YOU KNOW THAT NEVER WORKS! TO GET TO SPONGEBOB, YOU MUST SHOW HIM COMPASSION AND UNDERSTANDING.
WILL YOU BE QUIET! I'M THINKING! I'VE GOT IT!
TO GET TO SPONGEBOB, I'LL SHOW HIM COMPASSION AND UNDERSTANDING!
AND THEN HE'LL GIVE ME WHAT I WANT!

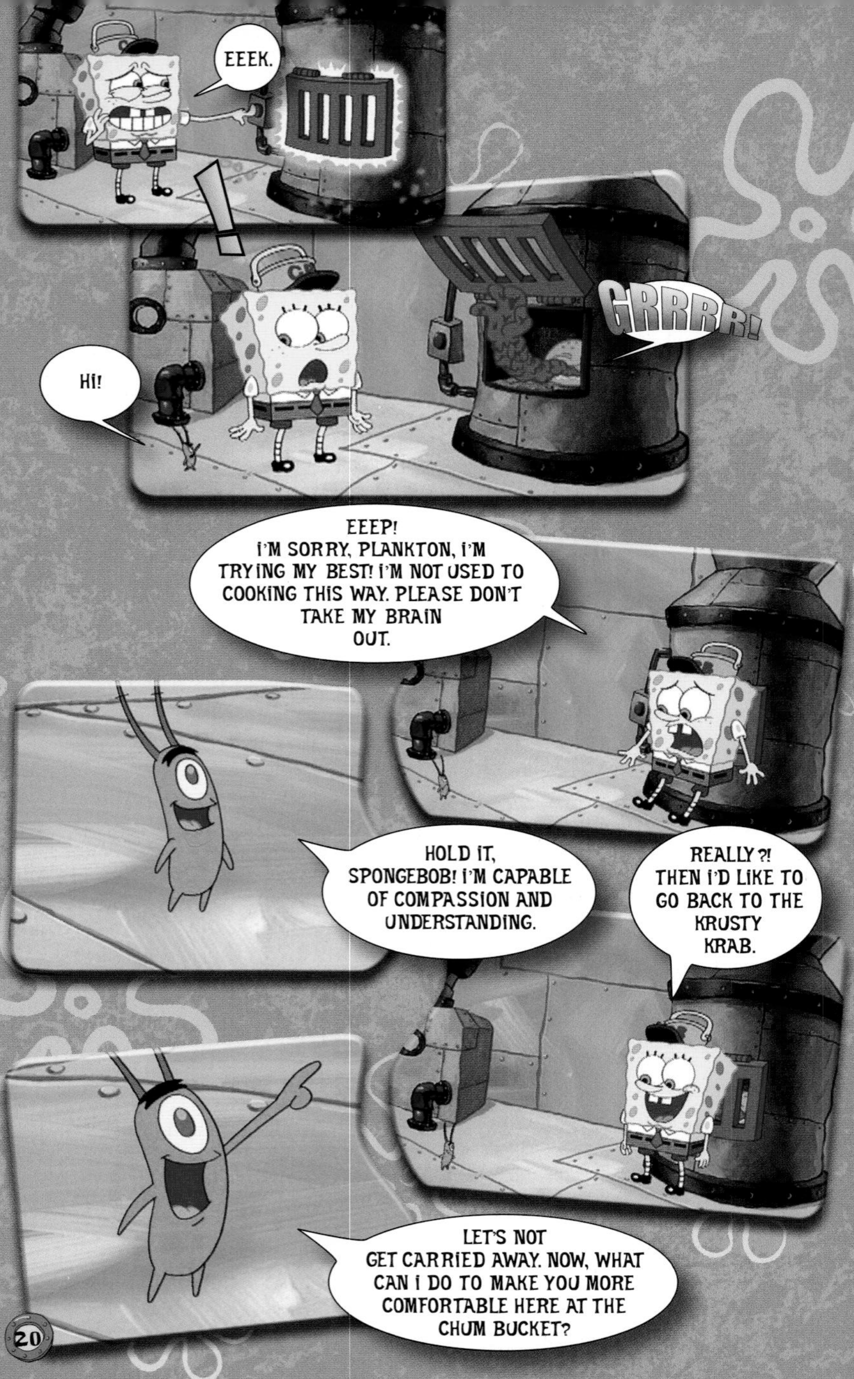

EEEK.
Hi!
GRRRR!
EEEP! I'M SORRY, PLANKTON, I'M TRYING MY BEST! I'M NOT USED TO COOKING THIS WAY. PLEASE DON'T TAKE MY BRAIN OUT.
HOLD IT, SPONGEBOB! I'M CAPABLE OF COMPASSION AND UNDERSTANDING.
REALLY?! THEN I'D LIKE TO GO BACK TO THE KRUSTY KRAB.
LET'S NOT GET CARRIED AWAY. NOW, WHAT CAN I DO TO MAKE YOU MORE COMFORTABLE HERE AT THE CHUM BUCKET?

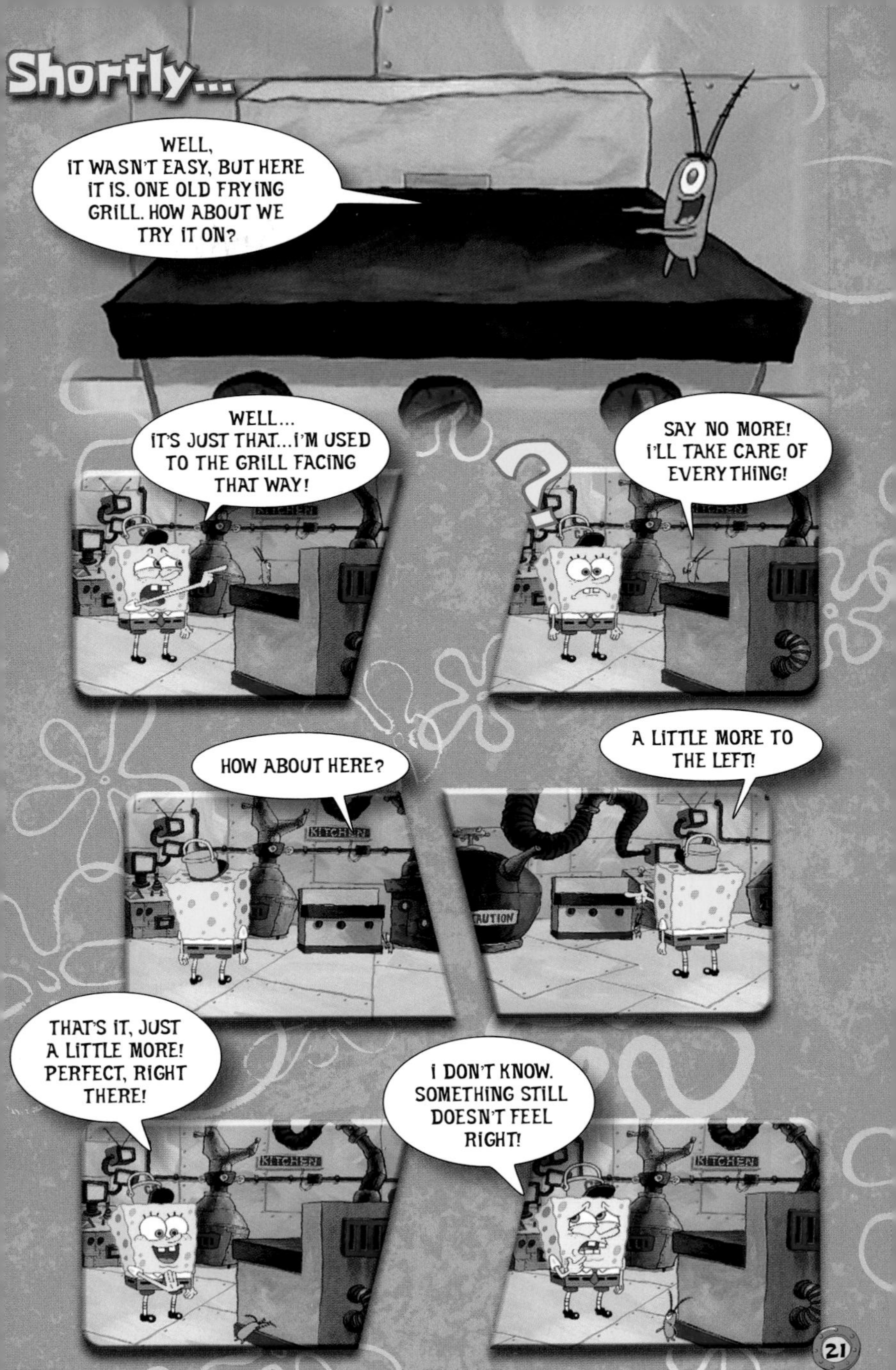
Shortly...
WELL, IT WASN'T EASY, BUT HERE IT IS. ONE OLD FRYING GRILL. HOW ABOUT WE TRY IT ON?
WELL... IT'S JUST THAT...I'M USED TO THE GRILL FACING THAT WAY!
SAY NO MORE! I'LL TAKE CARE OF EVERYTHING!
HOW ABOUT HERE?
A LITTLE MORE TO THE LEFT!
THAT'S IT, JUST A LITTLE MORE! PERFECT, RIGHT THERE!
I DON'T KNOW. SOMETHING STILL DOESN'T FEEL RIGHT!

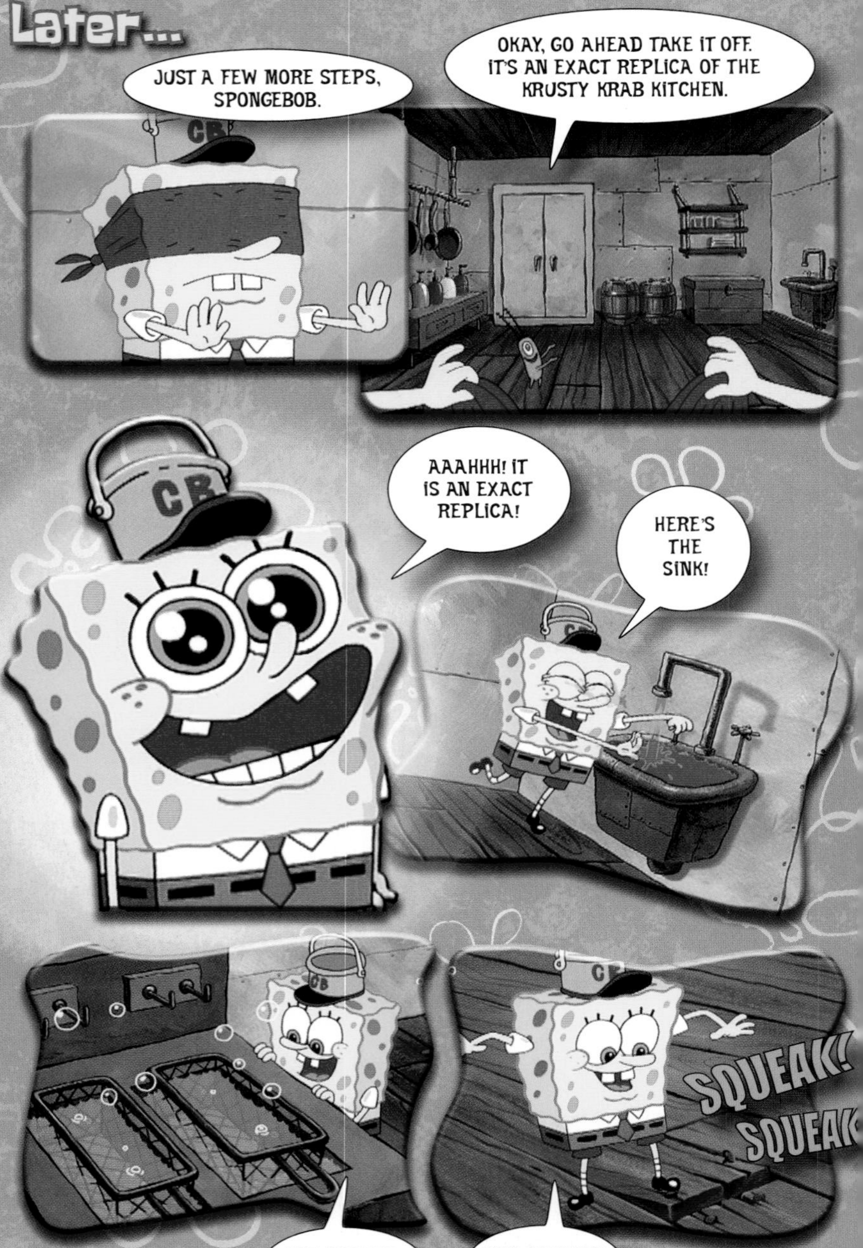
Later...
JUST A FEW MORE STEPS, SPONGEBOB.
OKAY, GO AHEAD TAKE IT OFF. IT'S AN EXACT REPLICA OF THE KRUSTY KRAB KITCHEN.
AAAHHH! IT IS AN EXACT REPLICA!
HERE'S THE SINK!
THE GREASY FRYERS!
THE SQUEAKY FLOORS!
SQUEAK!
SQUEAK

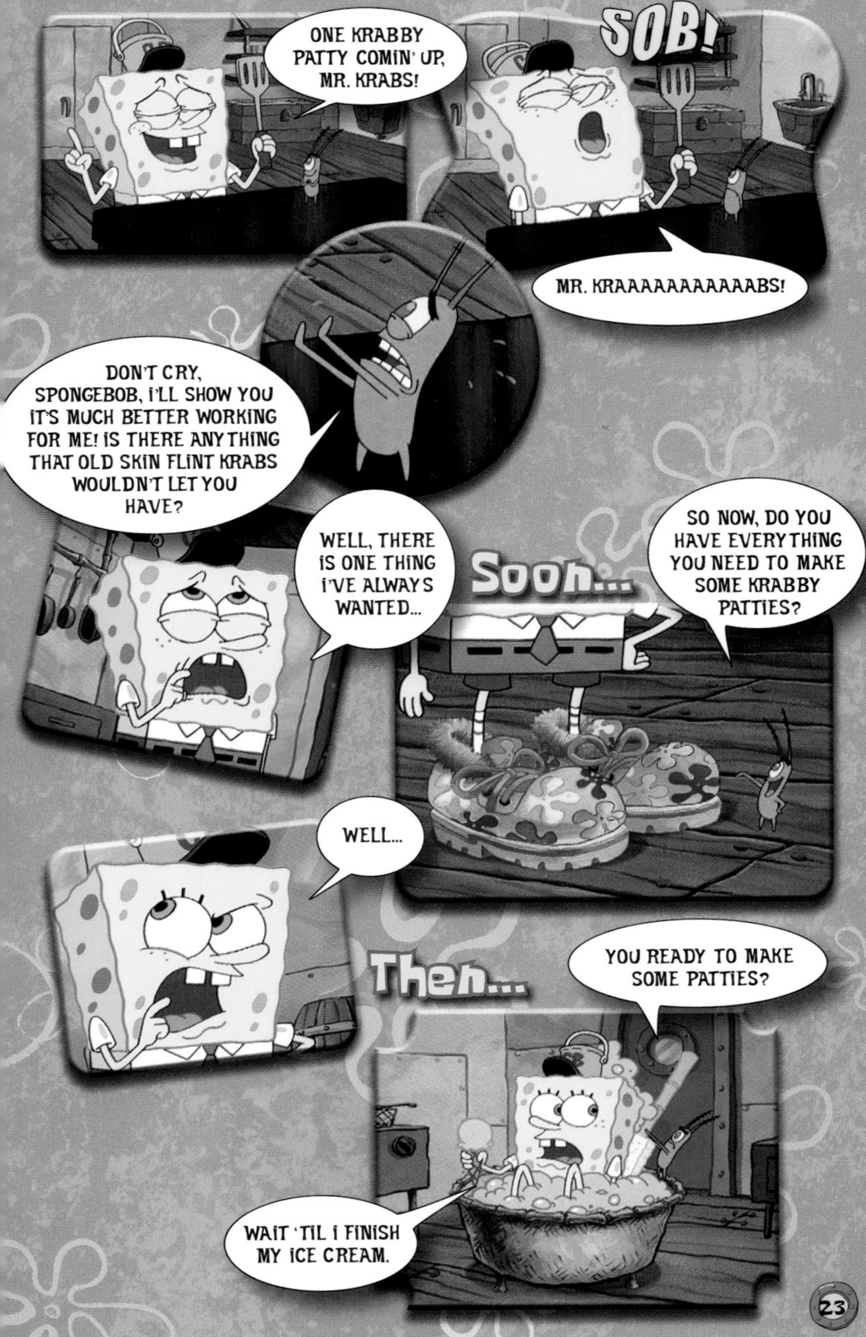
ONE KRABBY PATTY COMIN' UP, MR. KRABS!
SOB!
MR. KRAAAAAAAAAAABS!
DON'T CRY, SPONGEBOB, I'LL SHOW YOU IT'S MUCH BETTER WORKING FOR ME! IS THERE ANYTHING THAT OLD SKIN FLINT KRABS WOULDN'T LET YOU HAVE?
WELL, THERE IS ONE THING I'VE ALWAYS WANTED...
WELL...
Soon...
SO NOW, DO YOU HAVE EVERYTHING YOU NEED TO MAKE SOME KRABBY PATTIES?
Then...
YOU READY TO MAKE SOME PATTIES?
WAIT 'TIL I FINISH MY ICE CREAM.

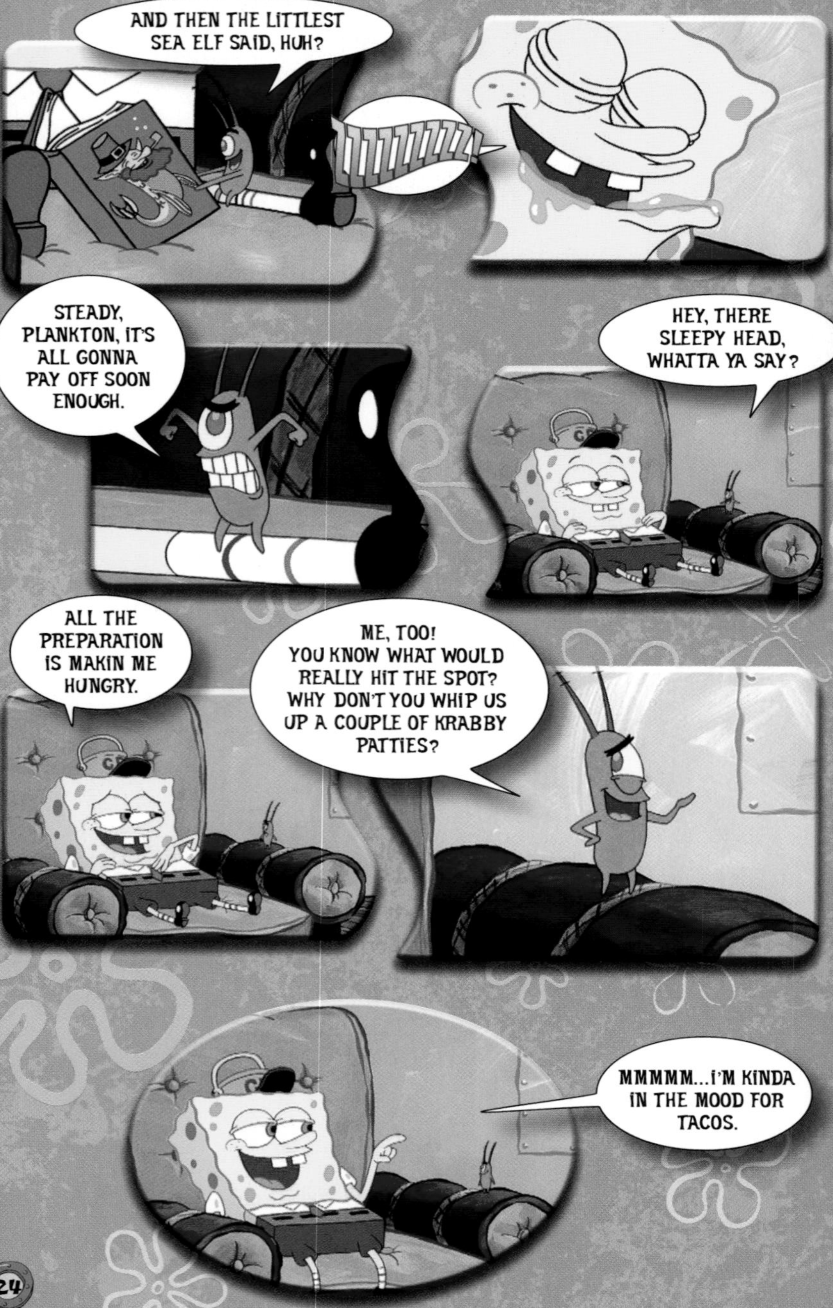
AND THEN THE LITTLEST SEA ELF SAID, HUH?
STEADY, PLANKTON, IT'S ALL GONNA PAY OFF SOON ENOUGH.
HEY, THERE SLEEPY HEAD, WHATTA YA SAY?
ALL THE PREPARATION IS MAKIN ME HUNGRY.
ME, TOO! YOU KNOW WHAT WOULD REALLY HIT THE SPOT? WHY DON'T YOU WHIP US UP A COUPLE OF KRABBY PATTIES?
MMMMM...I'M KINDA IN THE MOOD FOR TACOS.

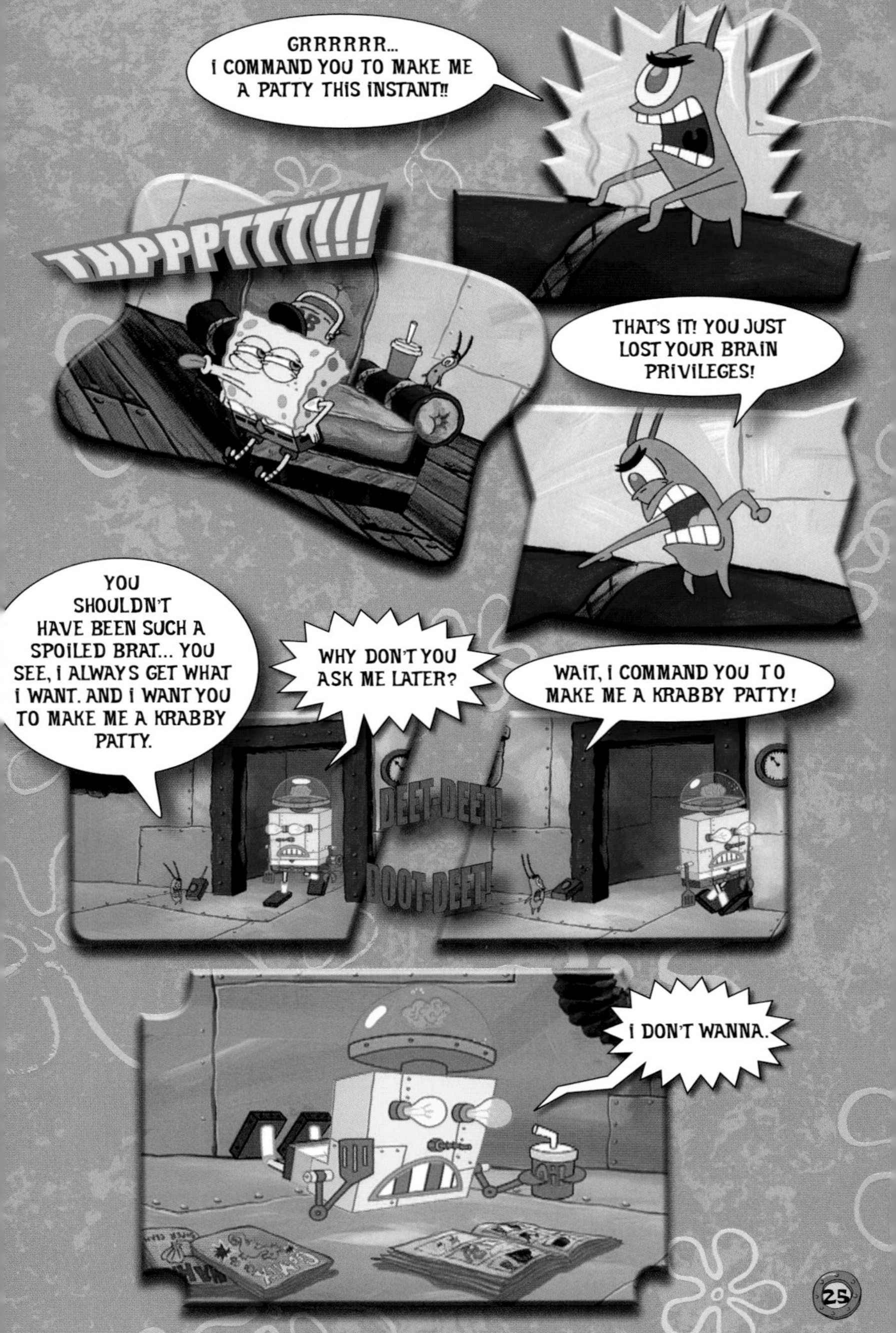

GRRRRRR... I COMMAND YOU TO MAKE ME A PATTY THIS INSTANT!!
THPPPTTTT!!!
THAT'S IT! YOU JUST LOST YOUR BRAIN PRIVILEGES!
YOU SHOULDN'T HAVE BEEN SUCH A SPOILED BRAT... YOU SEE, I ALWAYS GET WHAT I WANT. AND I WANT YOU TO MAKE ME A KRABBY PATTY.
WHY DON'T YOU ASK ME LATER?
DEET-DEET!
DOOT-DEET!
WAIT, I COMMAND YOU TO MAKE ME A KRABBY PATTY!
I DON'T WANNA.

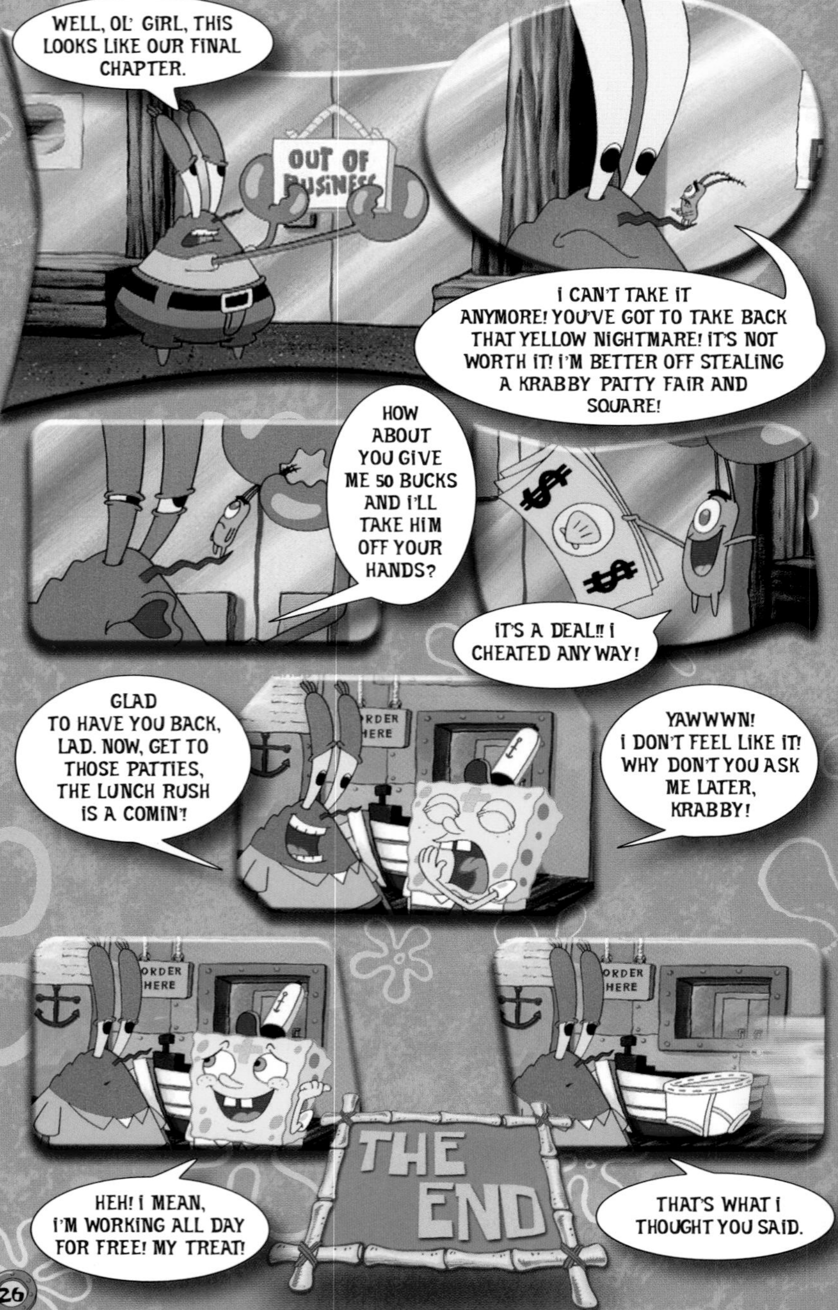
WELL, OL' GIRL, THIS LOOKS LIKE OUR FINAL CHAPTER.
OUT OF BUSINESS
I CAN'T TAKE IT ANYMORE! YOU'VE GOT TO TAKE BACK THAT YELLOW NIGHTMARE! IT'S NOT WORTH IT! I'M BETTER OFF STEALING A KRABBY PATTY FAIR AND SQUARE!
HOW ABOUT YOU GIVE ME 50 BUCKS AND I'LL TAKE HIM OFF YOUR HANDS?
IT'S A DEAL!! I CHEATED ANY WAY!
GLAD TO HAVE YOU BACK, LAD. NOW, GET TO THOSE PATTIES, THE LUNCH RUSH IS A COMIN'!
ORDER HERE
YAWWWN! I DON'T FEEL LIKE IT! WHY DON'T YOU ASK ME LATER, KRABBY!
ORDER HERE
ORDER HERE
HEH! I MEAN, I'M WORKING ALL DAY FOR FREE! MY TREAT!
THE END
THAT'S WHAT I THOUGHT YOU SAID.

SpongeBob SquarePants™

Patty Hype

By Jay Lender, Bill Reiss and Mr. Lawrence

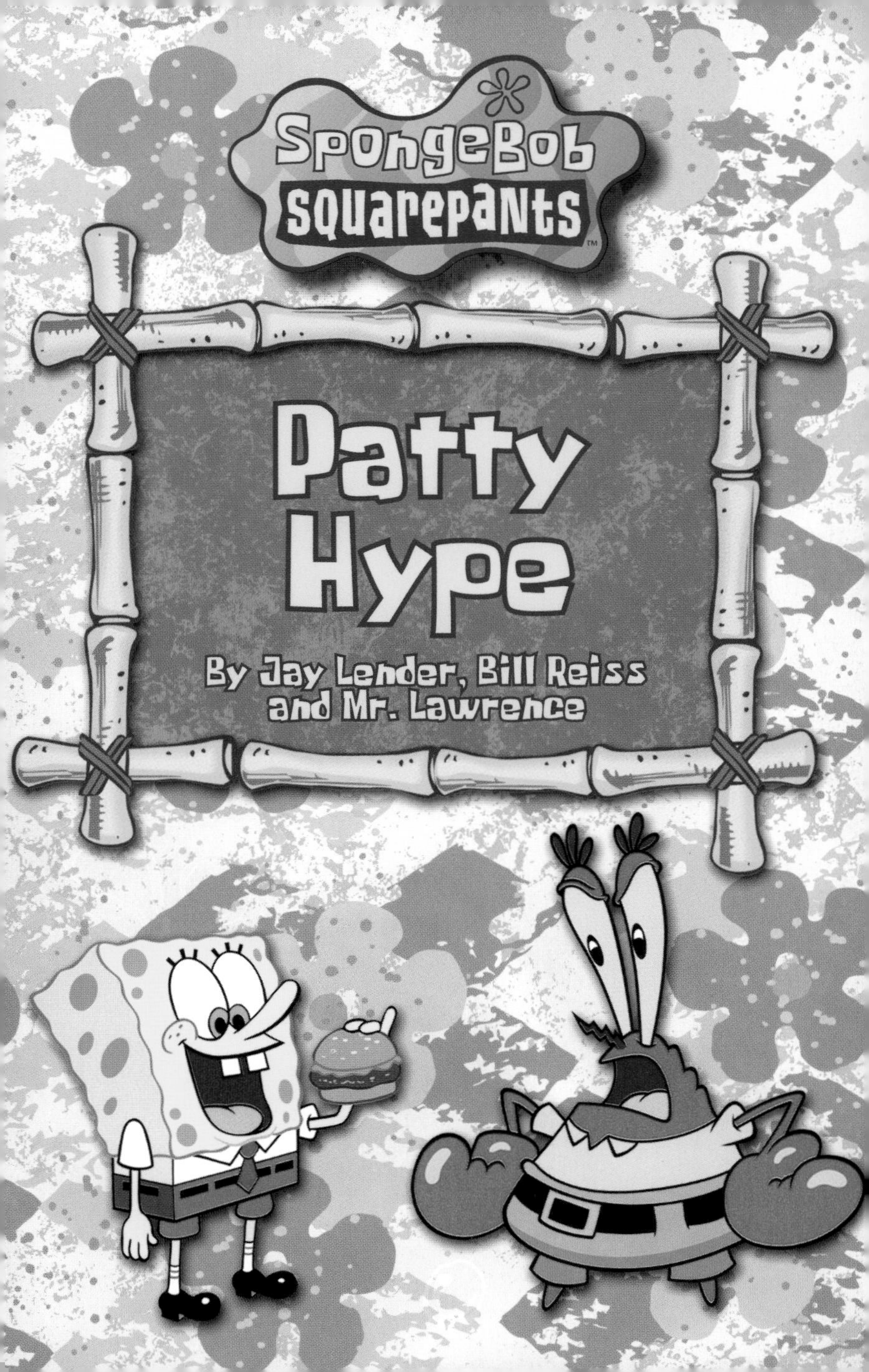

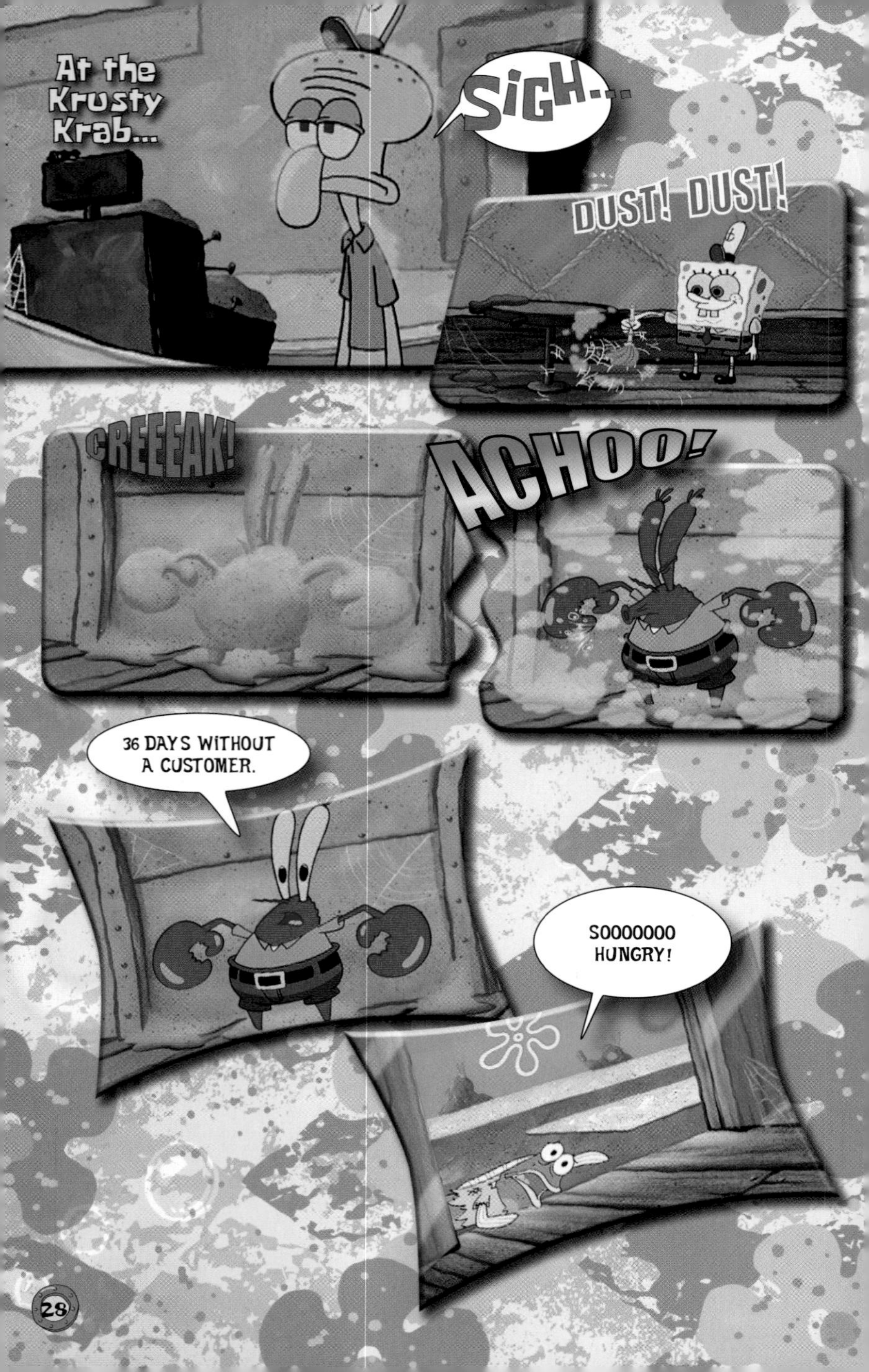

At the Krusty Krab...
SIGH...
DUST! DUST!
CREEEAK!
ACHOO!
36 DAYS WITHOUT A CUSTOMER.
SOOOOOOO HUNGRY!

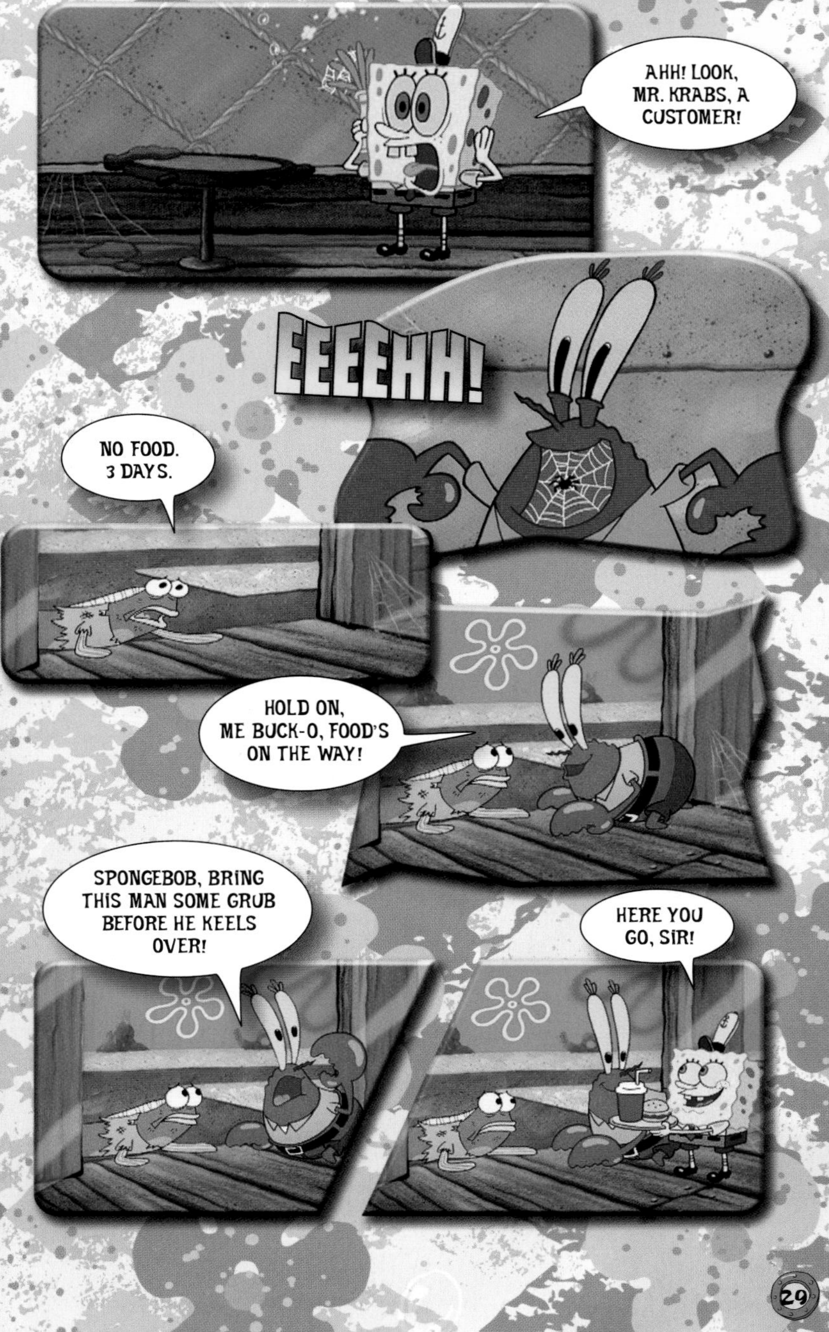
AHH! LOOK, MR. KRABS, A CUSTOMER!
EEEEHH!
NO FOOD. 3 DAYS.
HOLD ON, ME BUCK-O, FOOD'S ON THE WAY!
SPONGEBOB, BRING THIS MAN SOME GRUB BEFORE HE KEELS OVER!
HERE YOU GO, SIR!

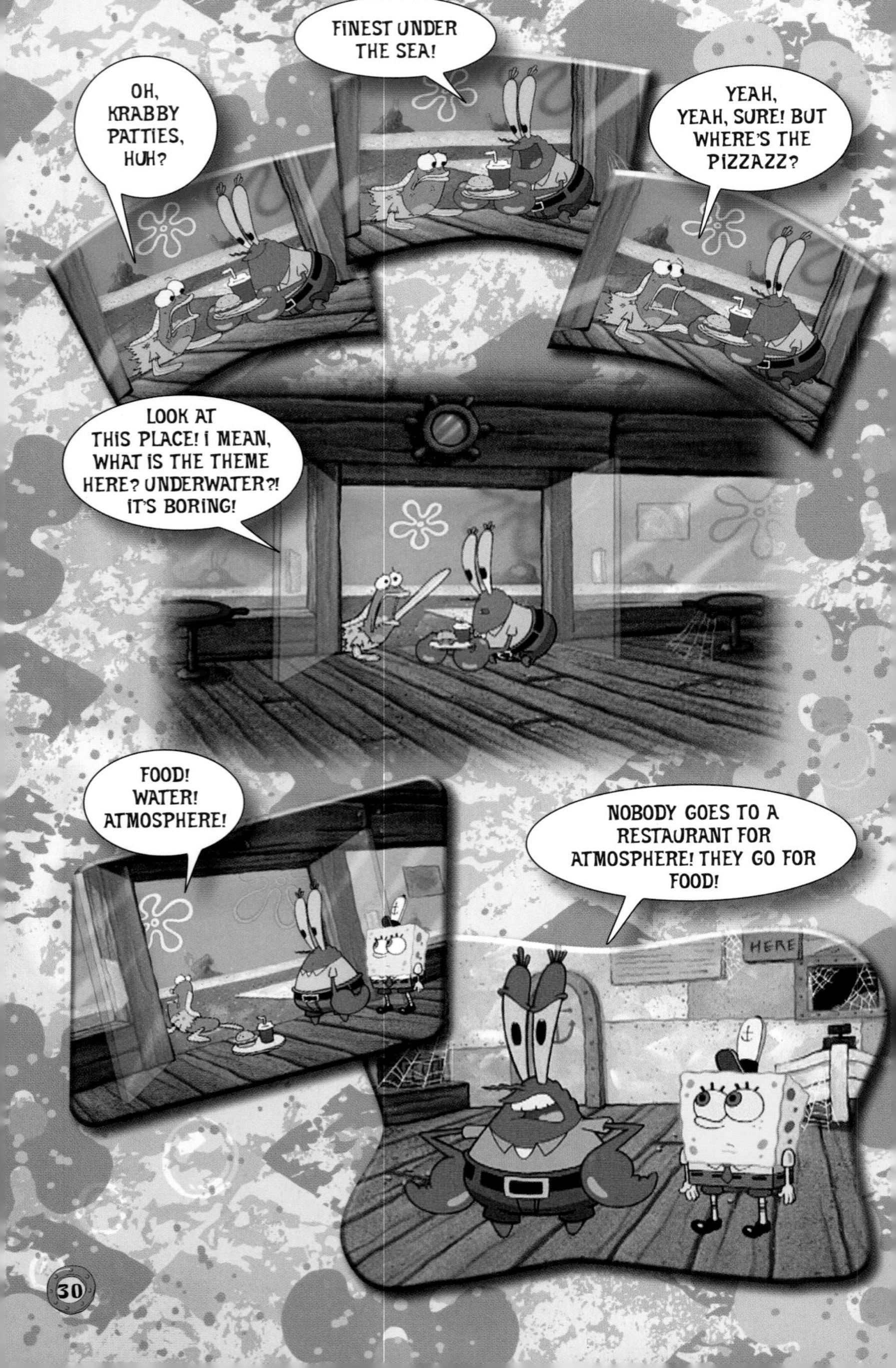
OH, KRABBY PATTIES, HUH?
FINEST UNDER THE SEA!
YEAH, YEAH, SURE! BUT WHERE'S THE PIZZAZZ?
LOOK AT THIS PLACE! I MEAN, WHAT IS THE THEME HERE? UNDERWATER?! IT'S BORING!
FOOD! WATER! ATMOSPHERE!
NOBODY GOES TO A RESTAURANT FOR ATMOSPHERE! THEY GO FOR FOOD!
HERE

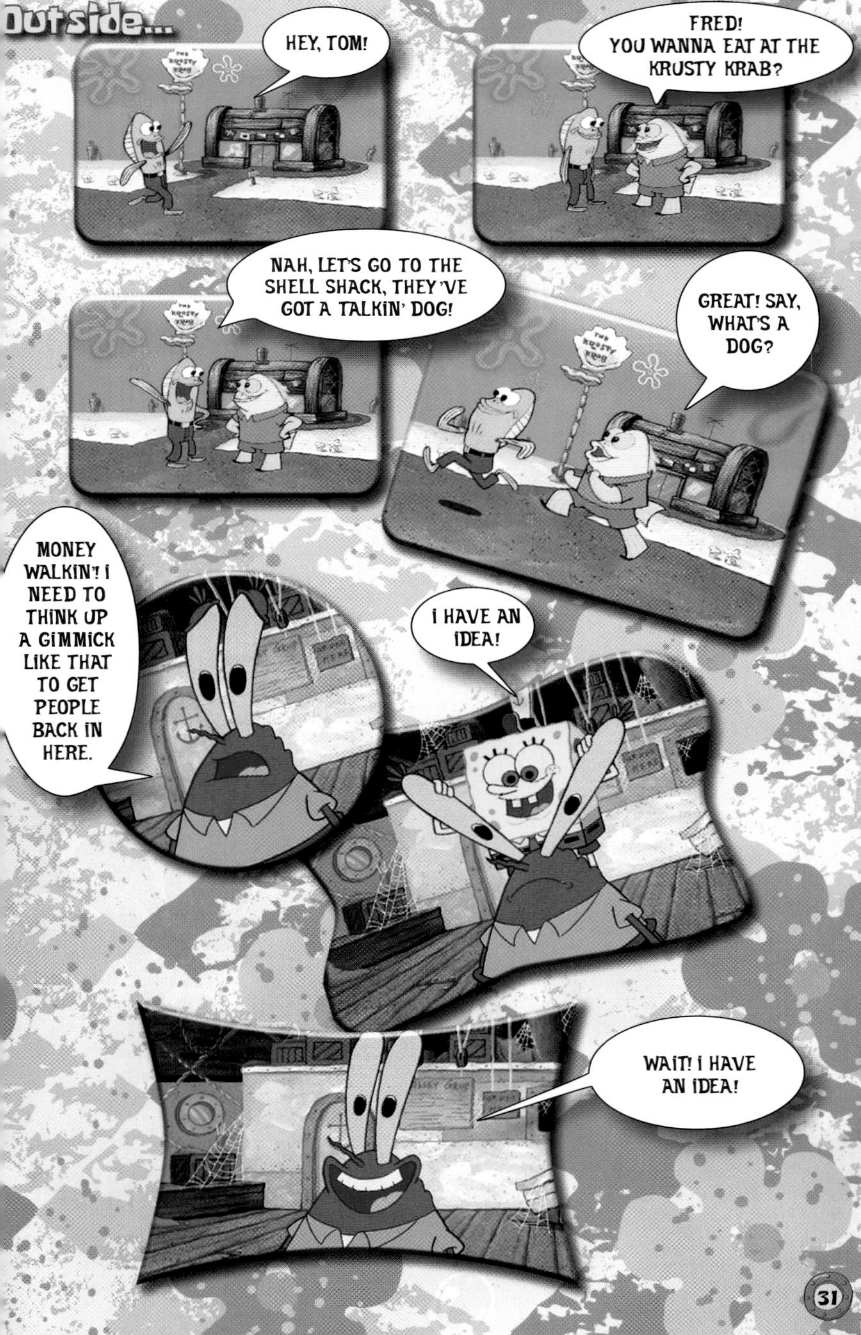
Outside...
HEY, TOM!
FRED! YOU WANNA EAT AT THE KRUSTY KRAB?
NAH, LET'S GO TO THE SHELL SHACK, THEY'VE GOT A TALKIN' DOG!
GREAT! SAY, WHAT'S A DOG?
MONEY WALKIN'! I NEED TO THINK UP A GIMMICK LIKE THAT TO GET PEOPLE BACK IN HERE.
I HAVE AN IDEA!
WAIT! I HAVE AN IDEA!

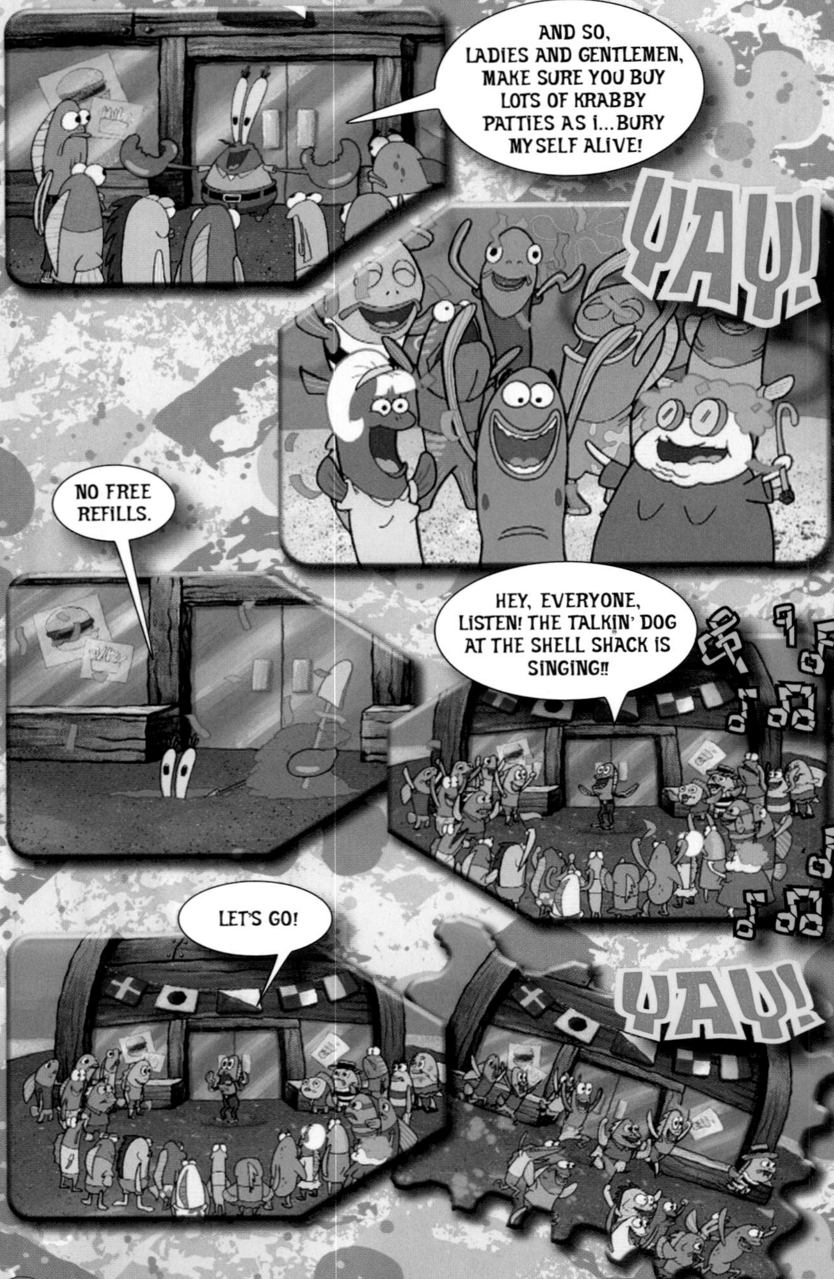
AND SO, LADIES AND GENTLEMEN, MAKE SURE YOU BUY LOTS OF KRABBY PATTIES AS I...BURY MYSELF ALIVE!
YAY!
NO FREE REFILLS.
HEY, EVERYONE, LISTEN! THE TALKIN' DOG AT THE SHELL SHACK IS SINGING!!
LET'S GO!
YAY!

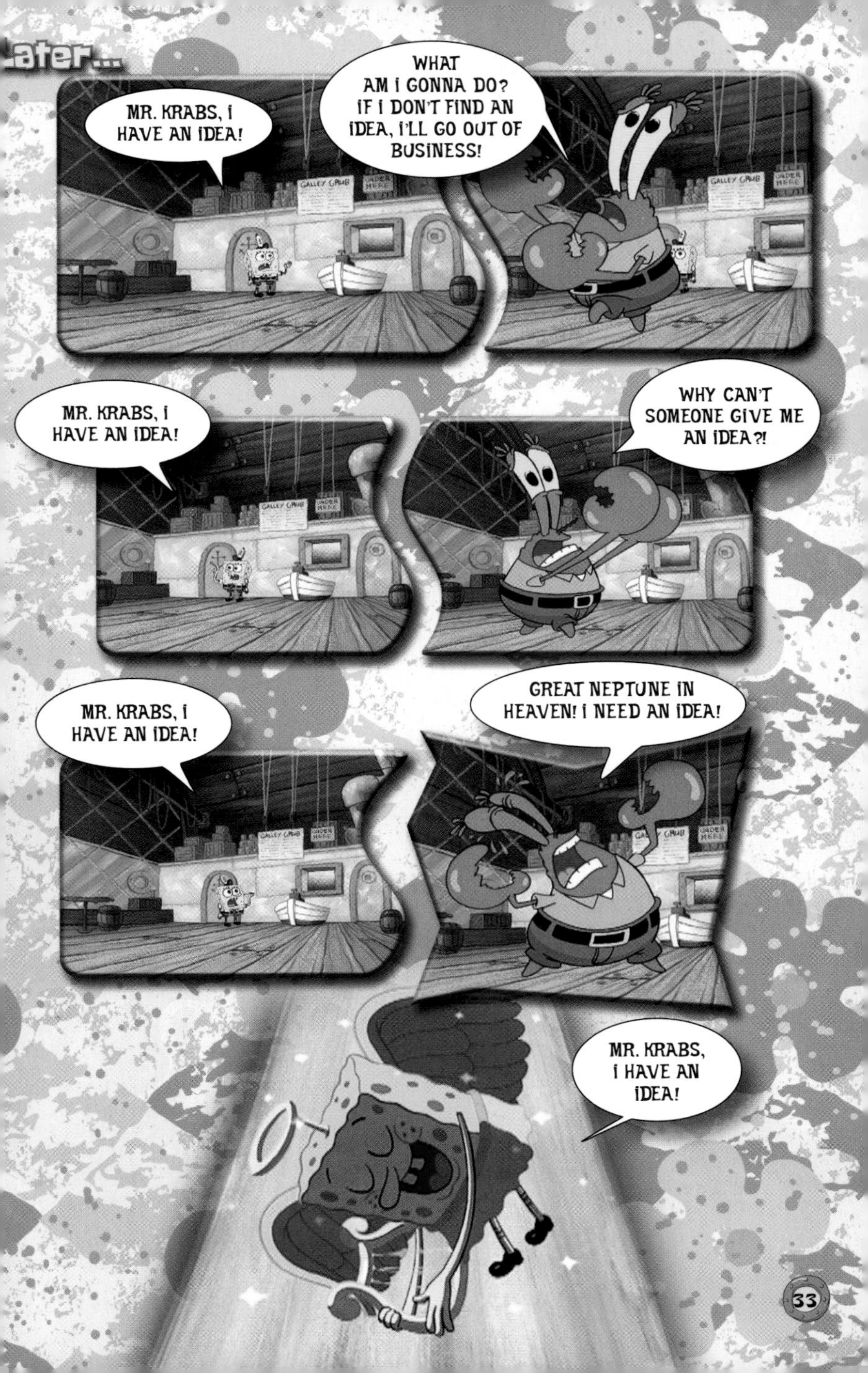
Later...
MR. KRABS, I HAVE AN IDEA!
WHAT AM I GONNA DO? IF I DON'T FIND AN IDEA, I'LL GO OUT OF BUSINESS!
MR. KRABS, I HAVE AN IDEA!
WHY CAN'T SOMEONE GIVE ME AN IDEA?!
MR. KRABS, I HAVE AN IDEA!
GREAT NEPTUNE IN HEAVEN! I NEED AN IDEA!
MR. KRABS, I HAVE AN IDEA!

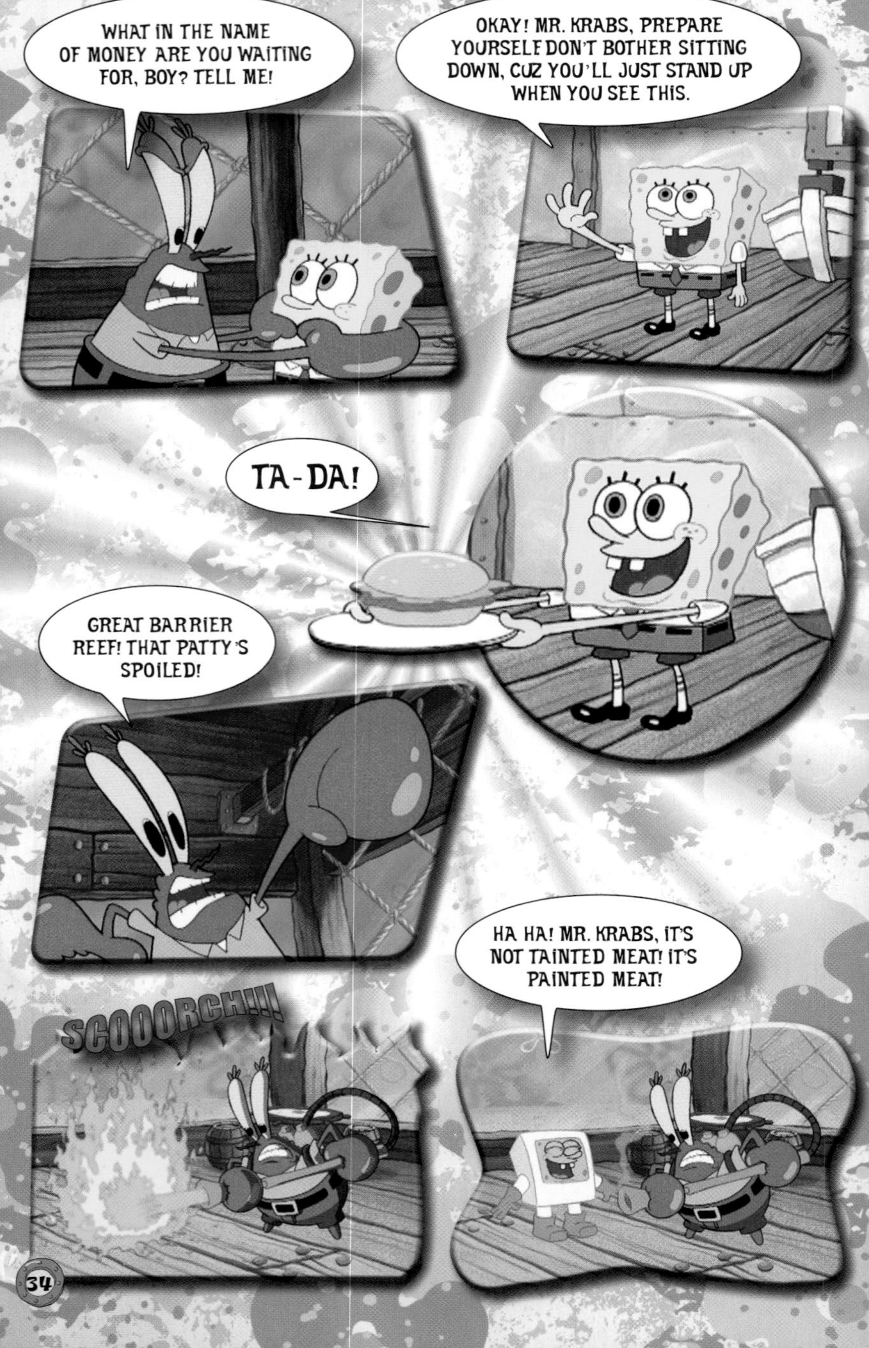

WHAT IN THE NAME OF MONEY ARE YOU WAITING FOR, BOY? TELL ME!
OKAY! MR. KRABS, PREPARE YOURSELF. DON'T BOTHER SITTING DOWN, CUZ YOU'LL JUST STAND UP WHEN YOU SEE THIS.
TA-DA!
GREAT BARRIER REEF! THAT PATTY'S SPOILED!
SCOOOORCH!!!
HA HA! MR. KRABS, IT'S NOT TAINTED MEAT! IT'S PAINTED MEAT!

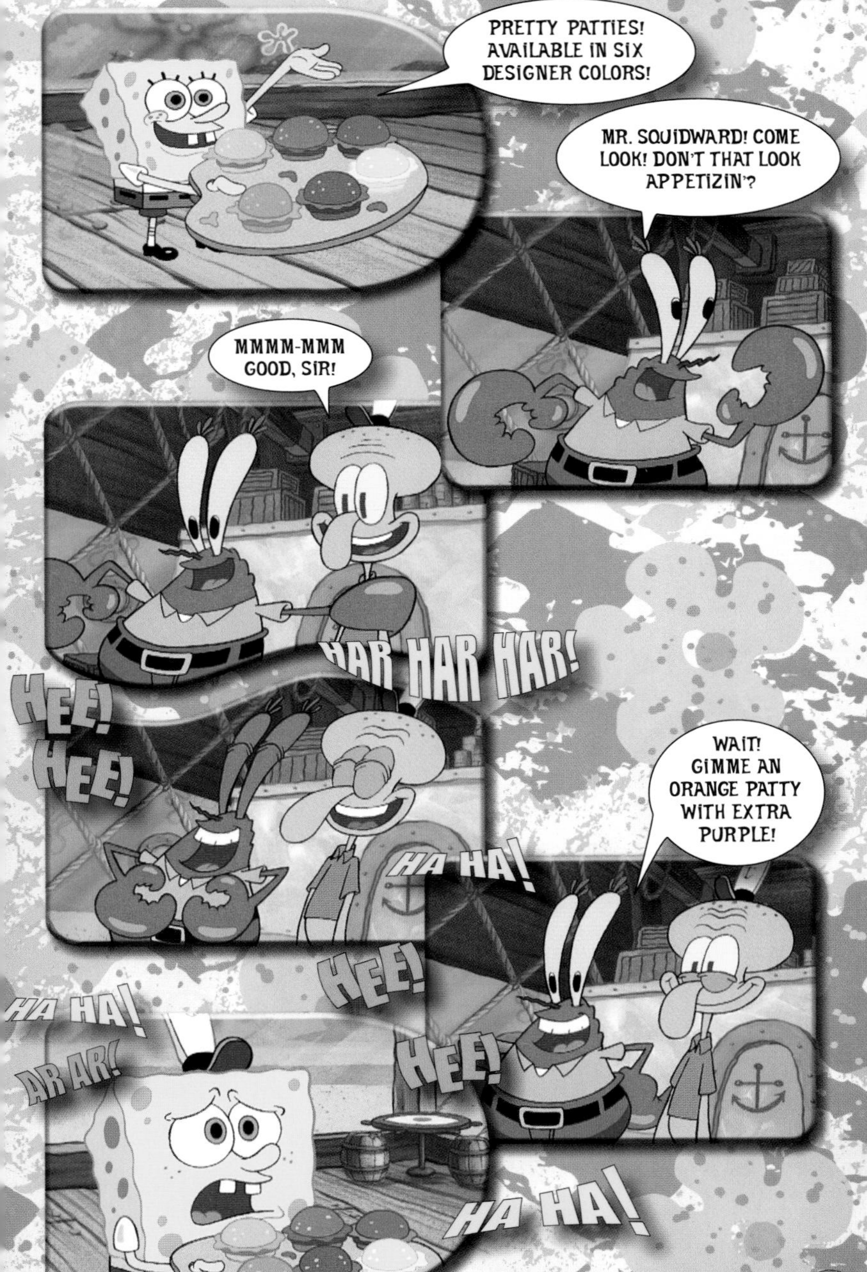
PRETTY PATTIES! AVAILABLE IN SIX DESIGNER COLORS!
MR. SQUIDWARD! COME LOOK! DON'T THAT LOOK APPETIZIN'?
MMMM-MMM GOOD, SIR!
HAR HAR HAR!
HEE! HEE!
HA HA!
WAIT! GIMME AN ORANGE PATTY WITH EXTRA PURPLE!
HEE!
HA HA!
AR AR!
HEE!
HA HA!

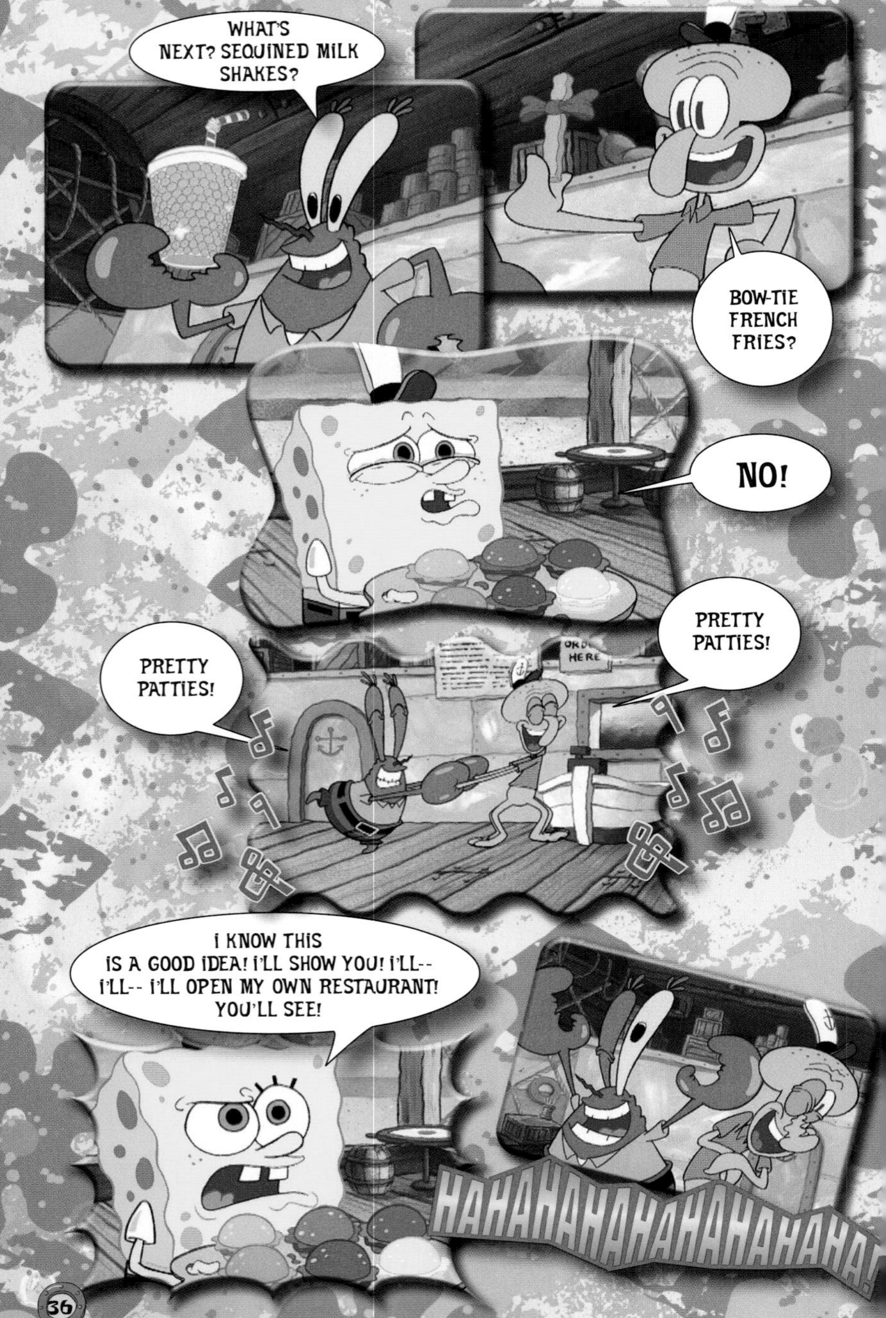
WHAT'S NEXT? SEQUINED MILK SHAKES?
BOW-TIE FRENCH FRIES?
NO!
PRETTY PATTIES!
PRETTY PATTIES!
I KNOW THIS IS A GOOD IDEA! I'LL SHOW YOU! I'LL-- I'LL-- I'LL OPEN MY OWN RESTAURANT! YOU'LL SEE!
HAHAHAHAHAHAHAHAHA!

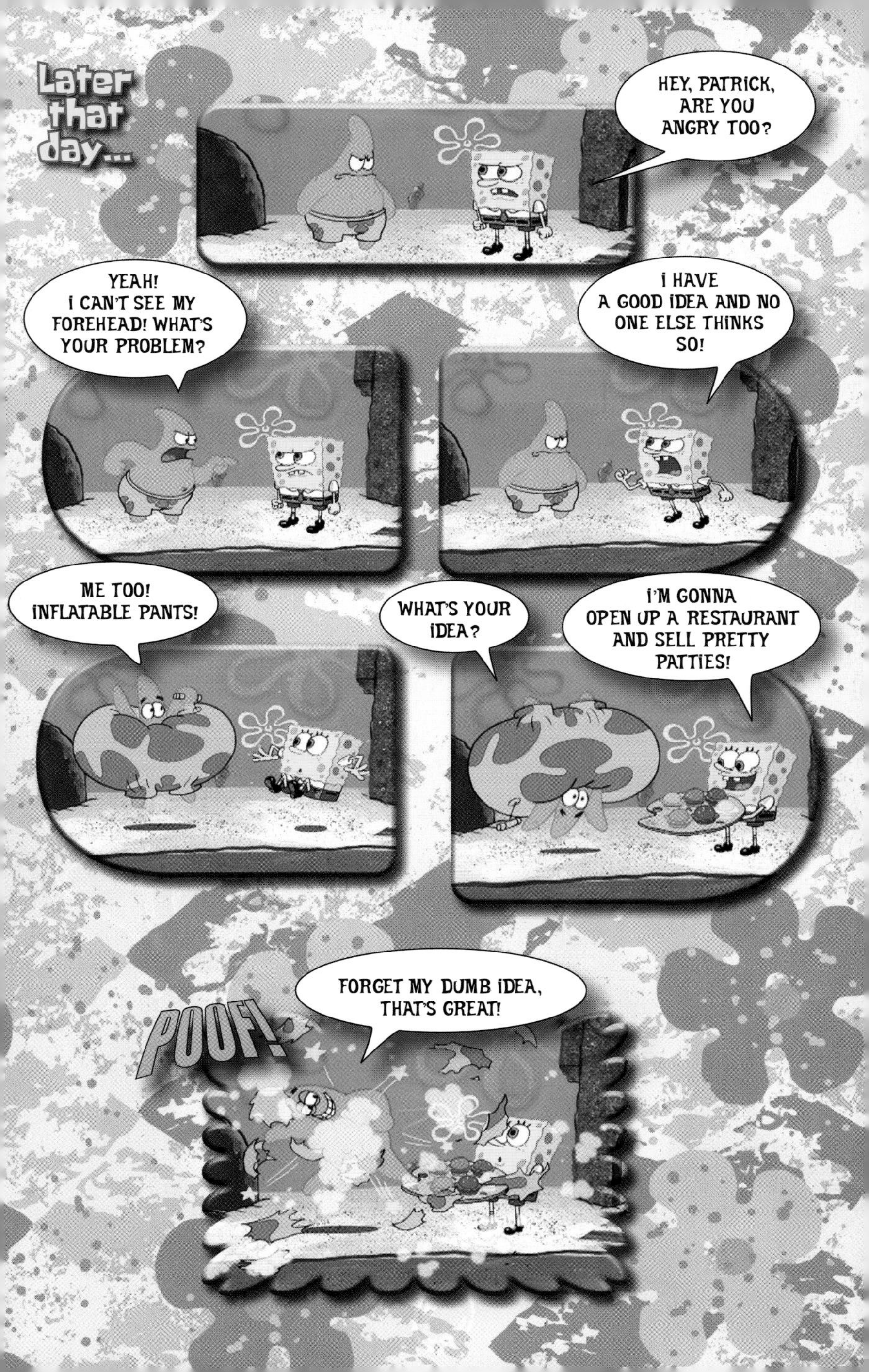
Later that day...
HEY, PATRICK, ARE YOU ANGRY TOO?
YEAH! I CAN'T SEE MY FOREHEAD! WHAT'S YOUR PROBLEM?
I HAVE A GOOD IDEA AND NO ONE ELSE THINKS SO!
ME TOO! INFLATABLE PANTS!
WHAT'S YOUR IDEA?
I'M GONNA OPEN UP A RESTAURANT AND SELL PRETTY PATTIES!
POOF!
FORGET MY DUMB IDEA, THAT'S GREAT!

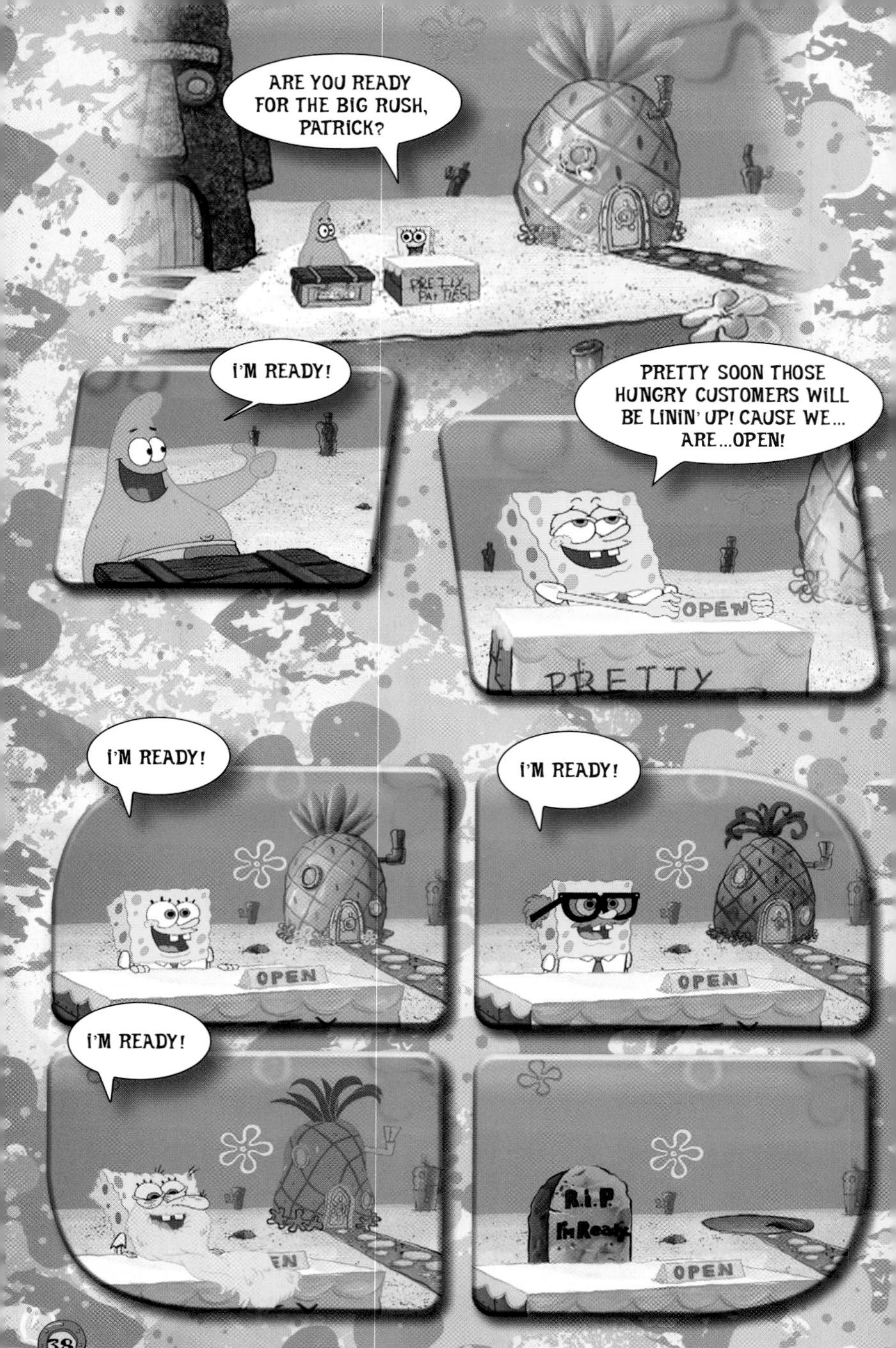
ARE YOU READY FOR THE BIG RUSH, PATRICK?
I'M READY!
PRETTY SOON THOSE HUNGRY CUSTOMERS WILL BE LININ' UP! CAUSE WE... ARE...OPEN!
OPEN
PRETTY
I'M READY!
OPEN
I'M READY!
OPEN
I'M READY!
R.I.P.
I'm Ready
OPEN

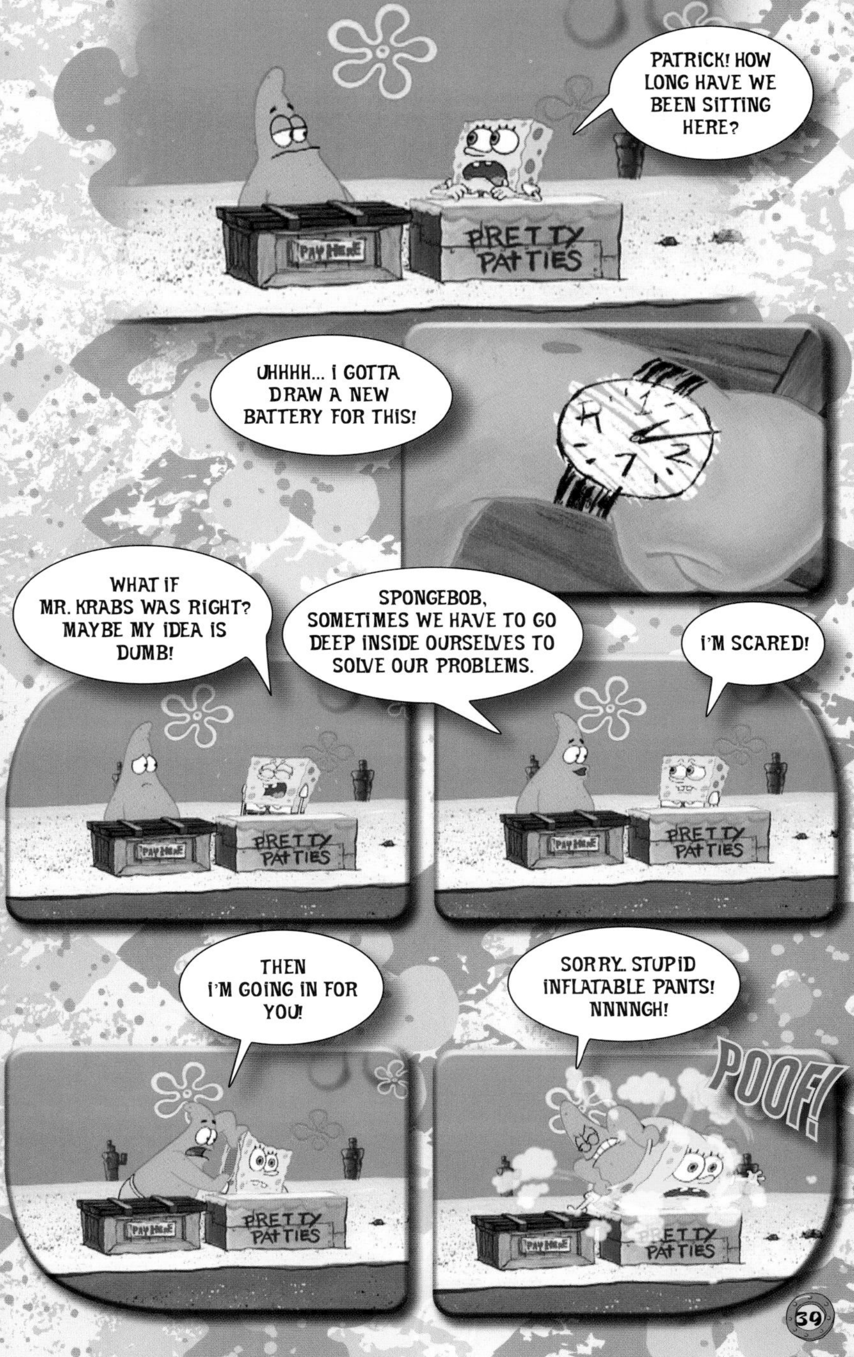
PATRICK! HOW LONG HAVE WE BEEN SITTING HERE?
PRETTY PATTIES
UHHHH... I GOTTA DRAW A NEW BATTERY FOR THIS!
WHAT IF MR. KRABS WAS RIGHT? MAYBE MY IDEA IS DUMB!
SPONGEBOB, SOMETIMES WE HAVE TO GO DEEP INSIDE OURSELVES TO SOLVE OUR PROBLEMS.
I'M SCARED!
THEN I'M GOING IN FOR YOU!
SORRY.. STUPID INFLATABLE PANTS! NNNNGH!
POOF!

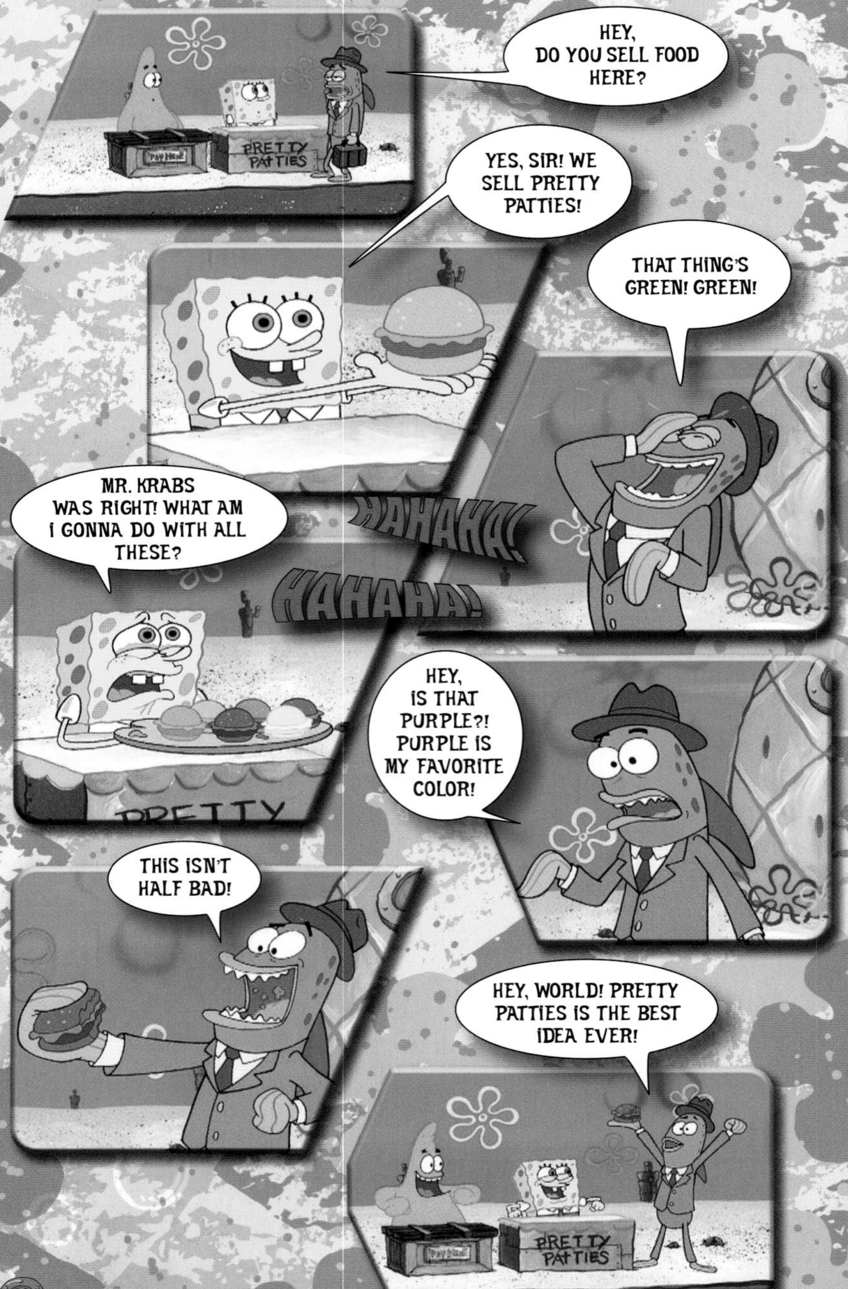
HEY, DO YOU SELL FOOD HERE?
PRETTY PATTIES
YES, SIR! WE SELL PRETTY PATTIES!
THAT THING'S GREEN! GREEN!
HAHAHA!
HAHAHA!
MR. KRABS WAS RIGHT! WHAT AM I GONNA DO WITH ALL THESE?
PRETTY
HEY, IS THAT PURPLE?! PURPLE IS MY FAVORITE COLOR!
THIS ISN'T HALF BAD!
HEY, WORLD! PRETTY PATTIES IS THE BEST IDEA EVER!
PRETTY PATTIES

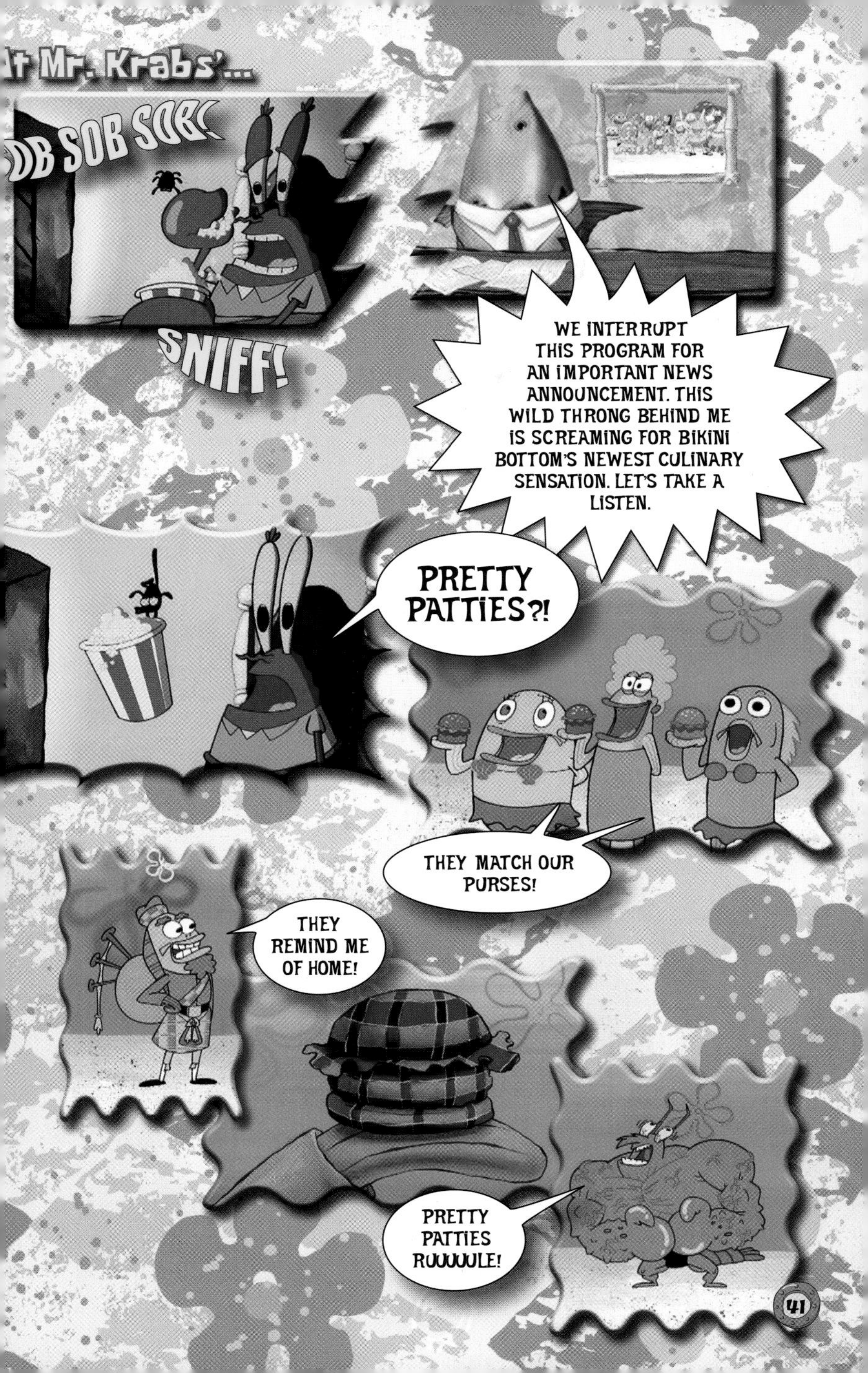
t Mr. Krabs'...
OB SOB SOB!
SNIFF!
WE INTERRUPT THIS PROGRAM FOR AN IMPORTANT NEWS ANNOUNCEMENT. THIS WILD THRONG BEHIND ME IS SCREAMING FOR BIKINI BOTTOM'S NEWEST CULINARY SENSATION. LET'S TAKE A LISTEN.
PRETTY PATTIES?!
THEY MATCH OUR PURSES!
THEY REMIND ME OF HOME!
PRETTY PATTIES RUUUUULE!

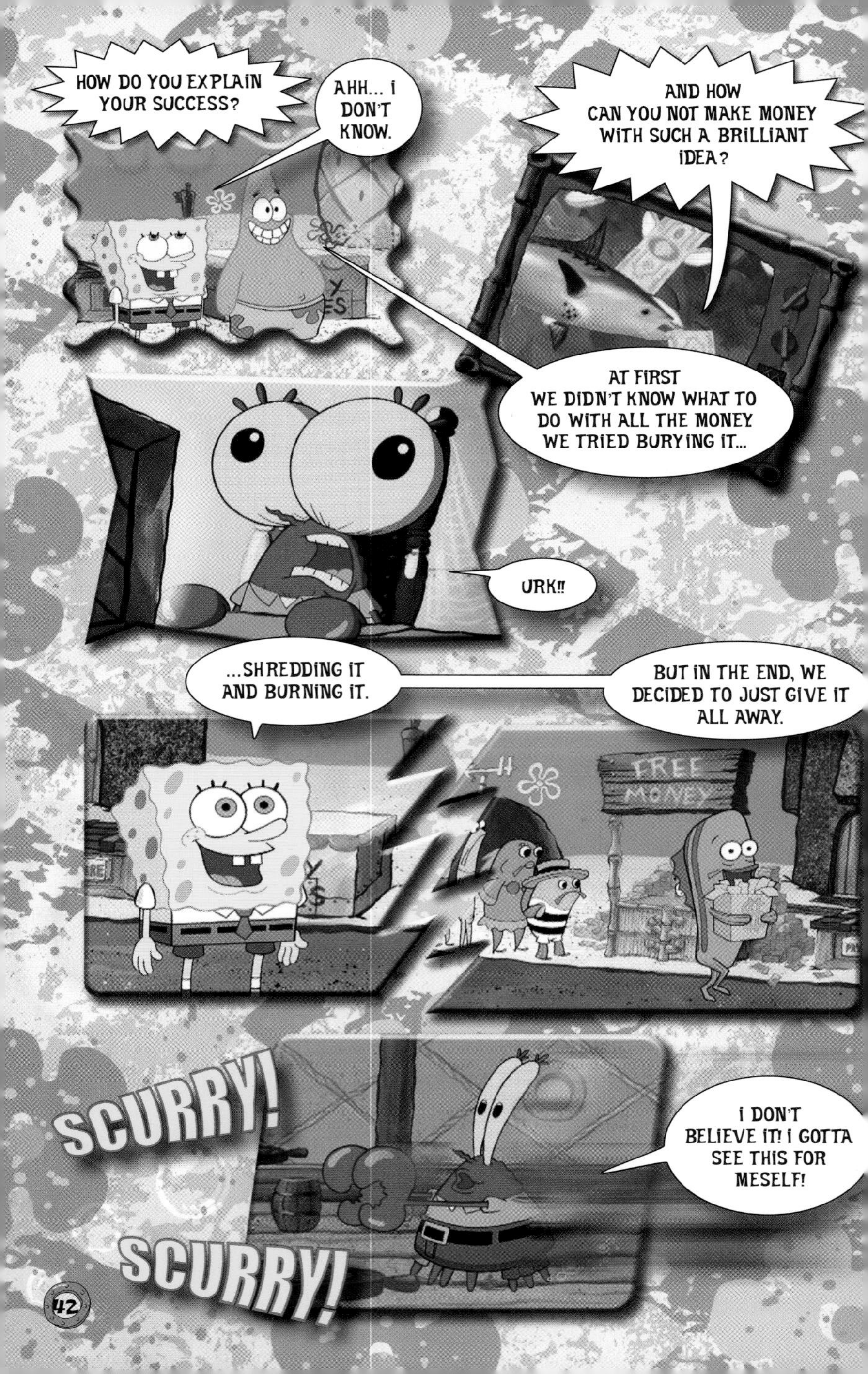
HOW DO YOU EXPLAIN YOUR SUCCESS?
AHH... I DON'T KNOW.
AND HOW CAN YOU NOT MAKE MONEY WITH SUCH A BRILLIANT IDEA?
AT FIRST WE DIDN'T KNOW WHAT TO DO WITH ALL THE MONEY. WE TRIED BURYING IT...
URK!!
...SHREDDING IT AND BURNING IT.
BUT IN THE END, WE DECIDED TO JUST GIVE IT ALL AWAY.
FREE MONEY
SCURRY!
SCURRY!
I DON'T BELIEVE IT! I GOTTA SEE THIS FOR MESELF!

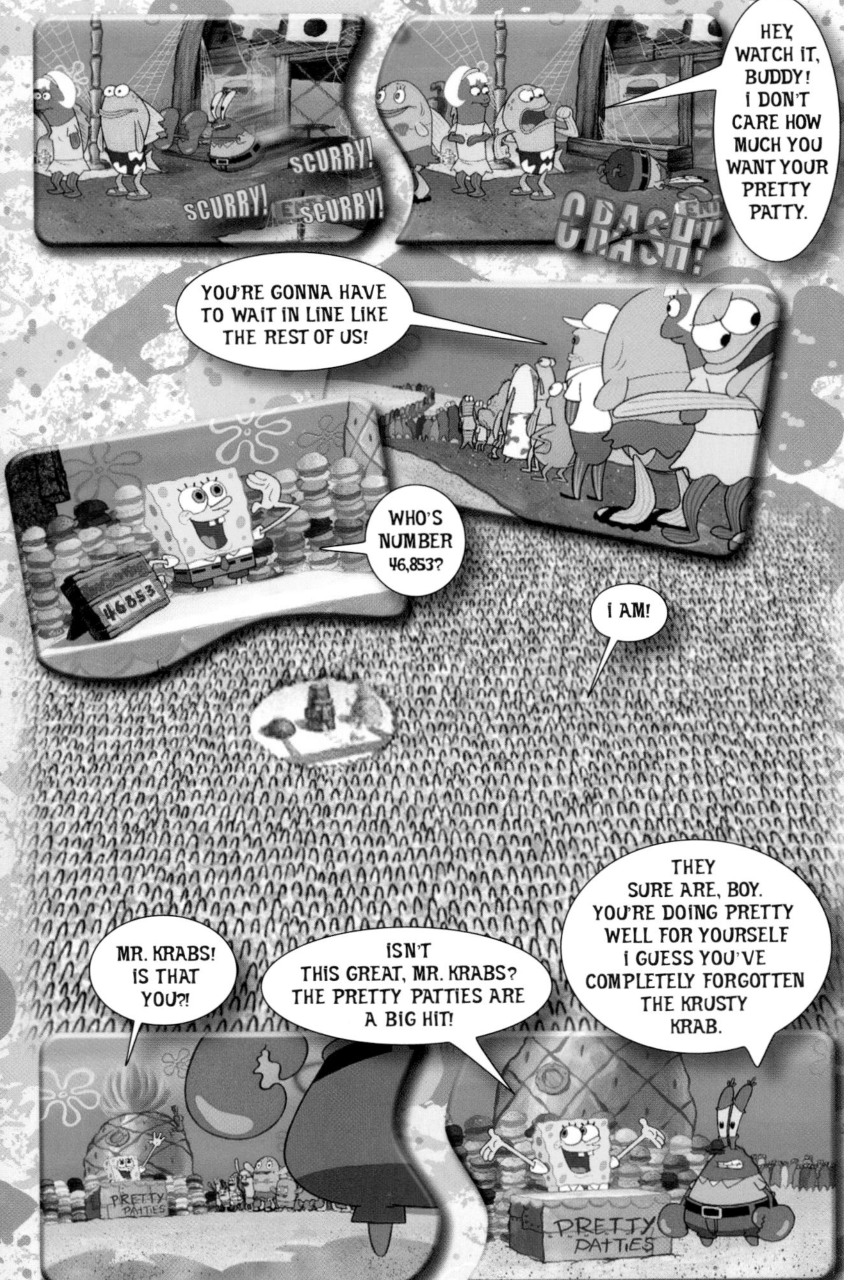
SCURRY!
SCURRY!
SCURRY!
CRASH!
HEY, WATCH IT, BUDDY! I DON'T CARE HOW MUCH YOU WANT YOUR PRETTY PATTY.
YOU'RE GONNA HAVE TO WAIT IN LINE LIKE THE REST OF US!
46853
WHO'S NUMBER 46,853?
I AM!
MR. KRABS! IS THAT YOU?!
PRETTY PATTIES
ISN'T THIS GREAT, MR. KRABS? THE PRETTY PATTIES ARE A BIG HIT!
THEY SURE ARE, BOY. YOU'RE DOING PRETTY WELL FOR YOURSELF. I GUESS YOU'VE COMPLETELY FORGOTTEN THE KRUSTY KRAB.
PRETTY PATTIES

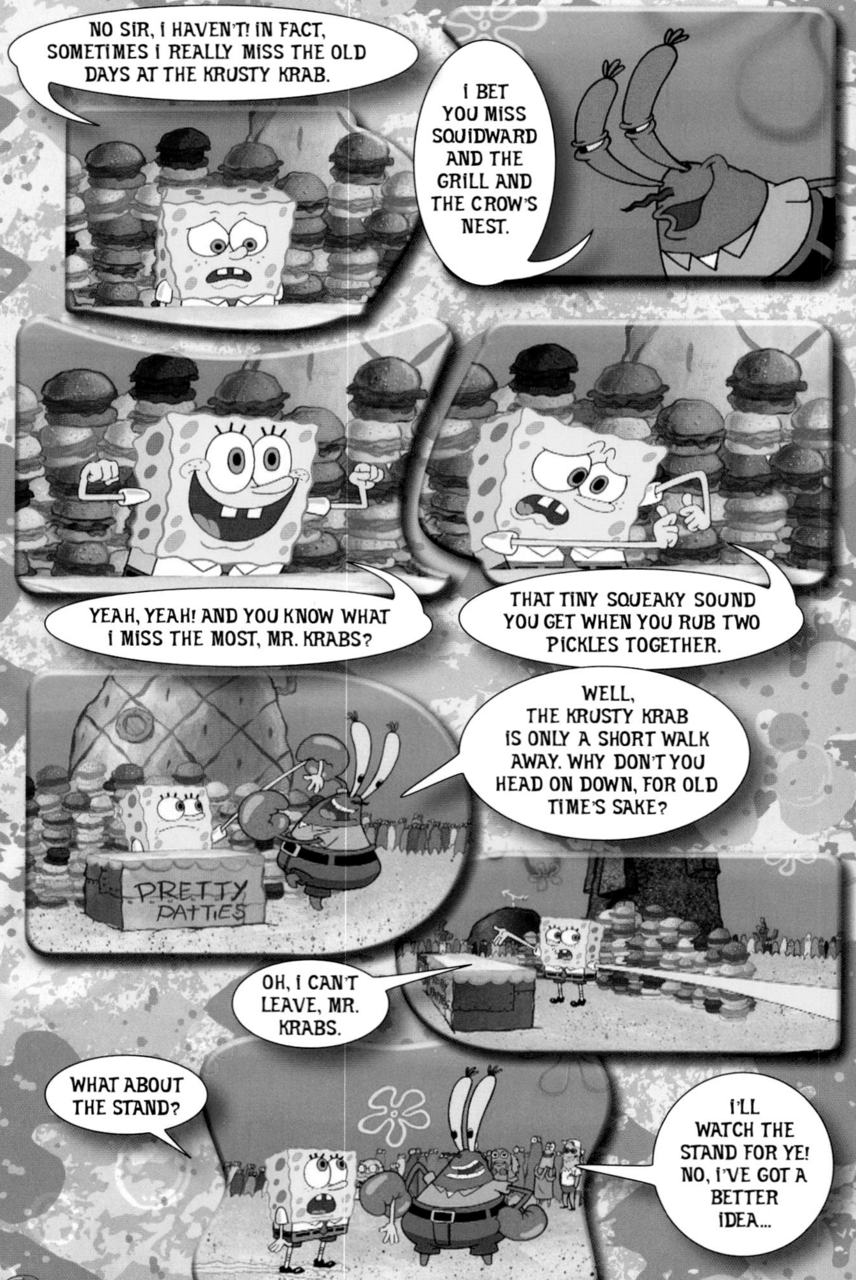

NO SIR, I HAVEN'T! IN FACT, SOMETIMES I REALLY MISS THE OLD DAYS AT THE KRUSTY KRAB.
I BET YOU MISS SQUIDWARD AND THE GRILL AND THE CROW'S NEST.
YEAH, YEAH! AND YOU KNOW WHAT I MISS THE MOST, MR. KRABS?
THAT TINY SQUEAKY SOUND YOU GET WHEN YOU RUB TWO PICKLES TOGETHER.
PRETTY PATTIES
WELL, THE KRUSTY KRAB IS ONLY A SHORT WALK AWAY. WHY DON'T YOU HEAD ON DOWN, FOR OLD TIME'S SAKE?
OH, I CAN'T LEAVE, MR. KRABS.
WHAT ABOUT THE STAND?
I'LL WATCH THE STAND FOR YE! NO, I'VE GOT A BETTER IDEA...

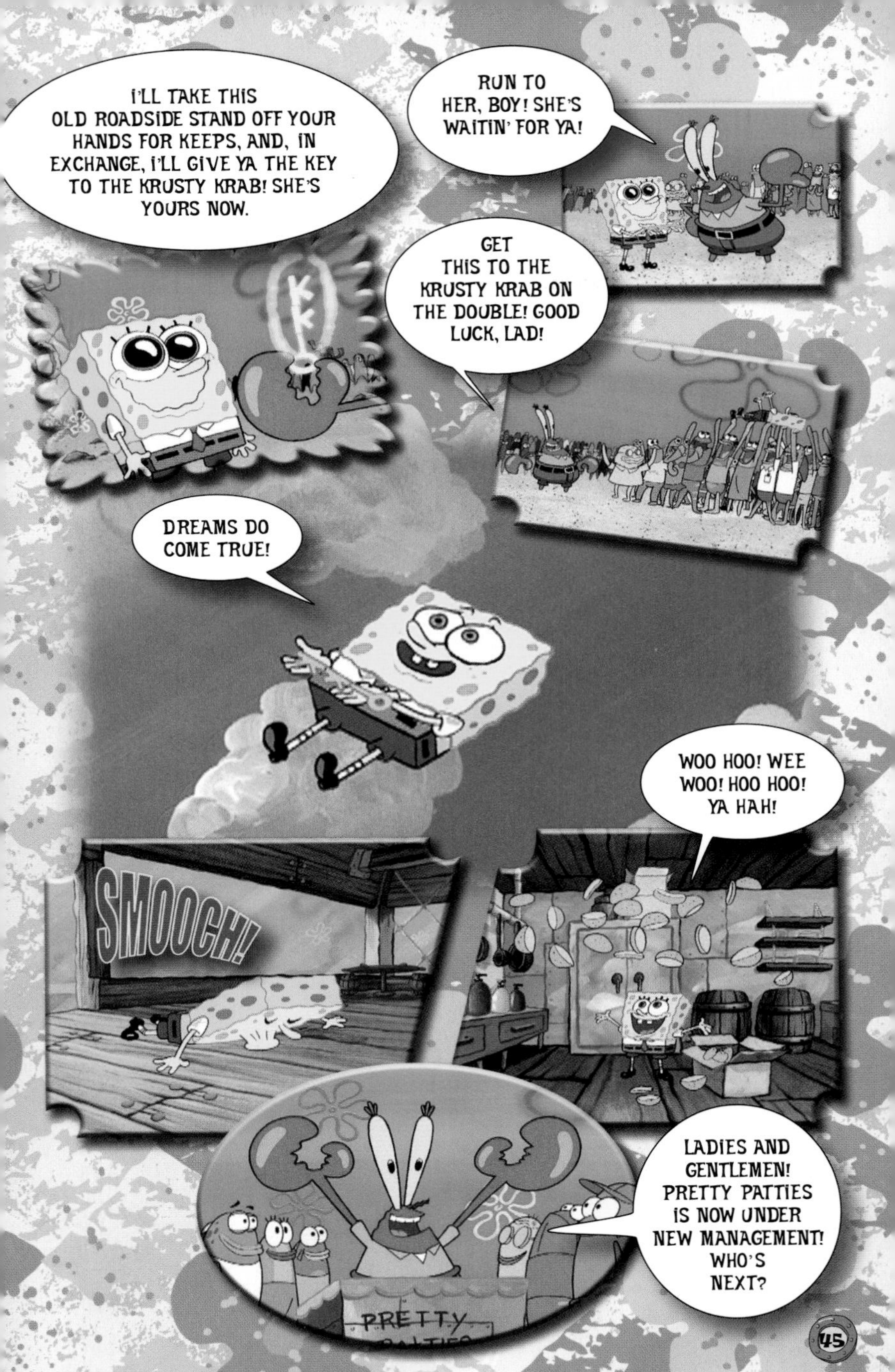
I'LL TAKE THIS OLD ROADSIDE STAND OFF YOUR HANDS FOR KEEPS, AND, IN EXCHANGE, I'LL GIVE YA THE KEY TO THE KRUSTY KRAB! SHE'S YOURS NOW.
RUN TO HER, BOY! SHE'S WAITIN' FOR YA!
GET THIS TO THE KRUSTY KRAB ON THE DOUBLE! GOOD LUCK, LAD!
DREAMS DO COME TRUE!
SMOOCH!
WOO HOO! WEE WOO! HOO HOO! YA HAH!
LADIES AND GENTLEMEN! PRETTY PATTIES IS NOW UNDER NEW MANAGEMENT! WHO'S NEXT?
PRETTY

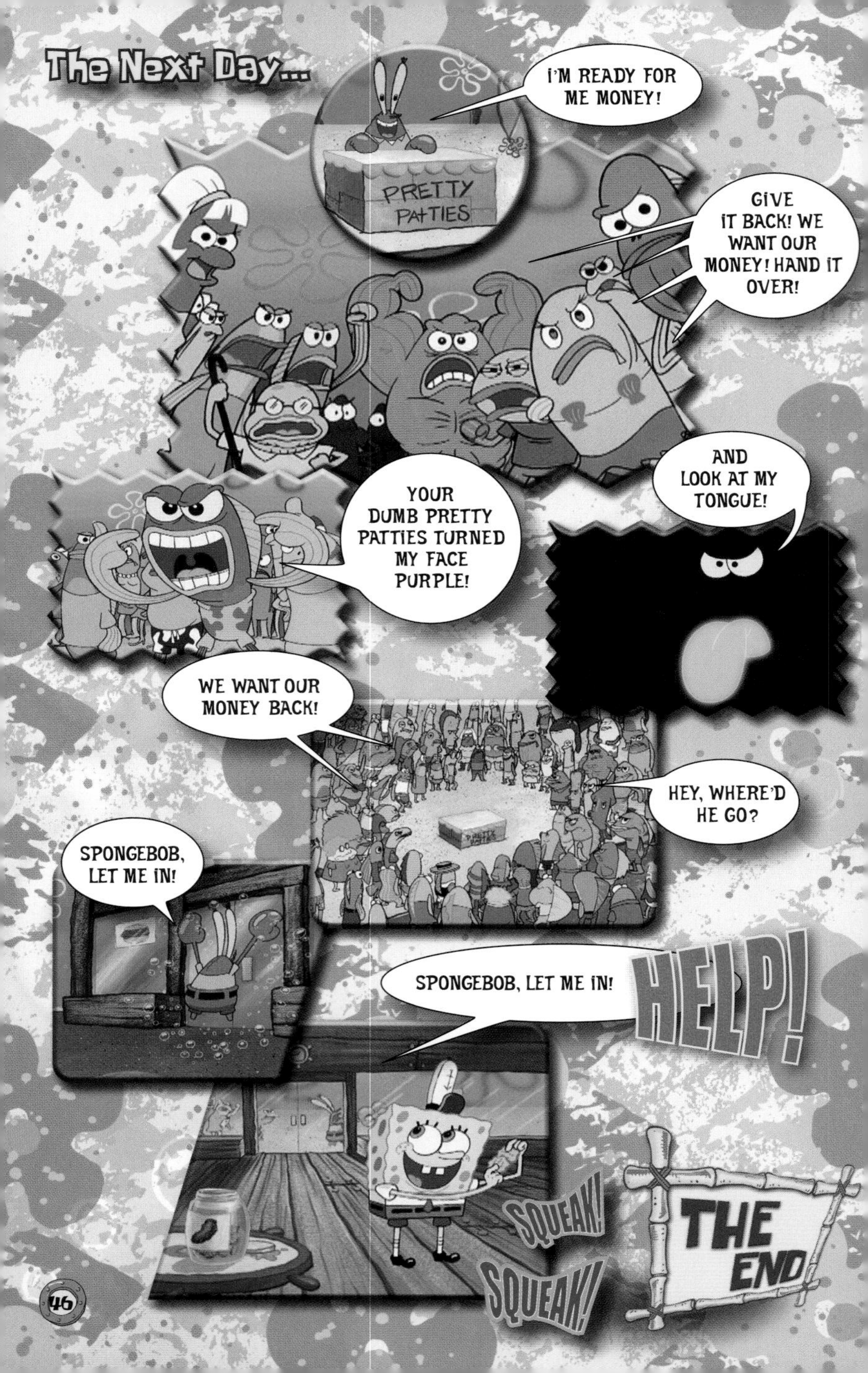
The Next Day...
I'M READY FOR ME MONEY!
PRETTY PATTIES
GIVE IT BACK! WE WANT OUR MONEY! HAND IT OVER!
YOUR DUMB PRETTY PATTIES TURNED MY FACE PURPLE!
AND LOOK AT MY TONGUE!
WE WANT OUR MONEY BACK!
HEY, WHERE'D HE GO?
SPONGEBOB, LET ME IN!
SPONGEBOB, LET ME IN!
HELP!
SQUEAK!
SQUEAK!
THE END

SpongeBob SquarePants

Dying For Pie

By Aaron Springer, C.H. Greenblatt and Merriweather Williams

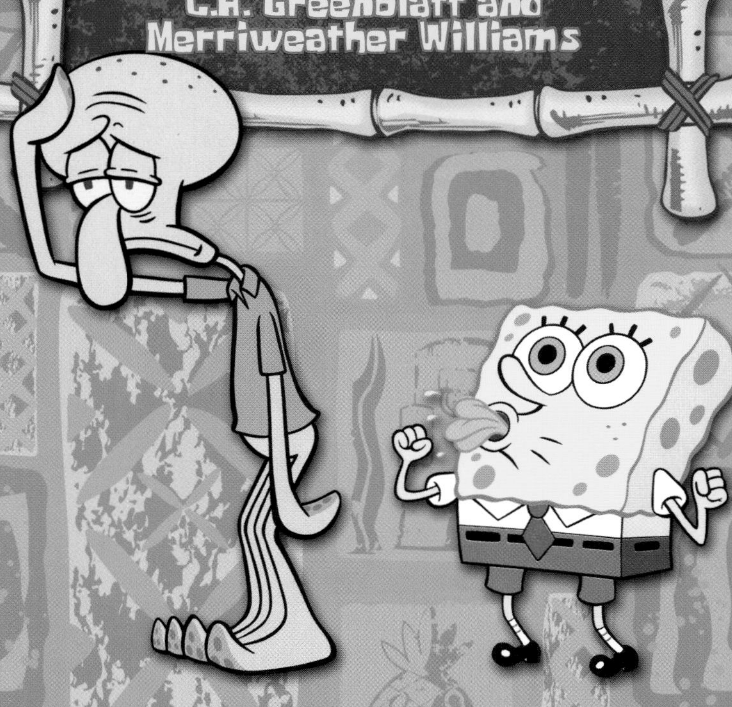

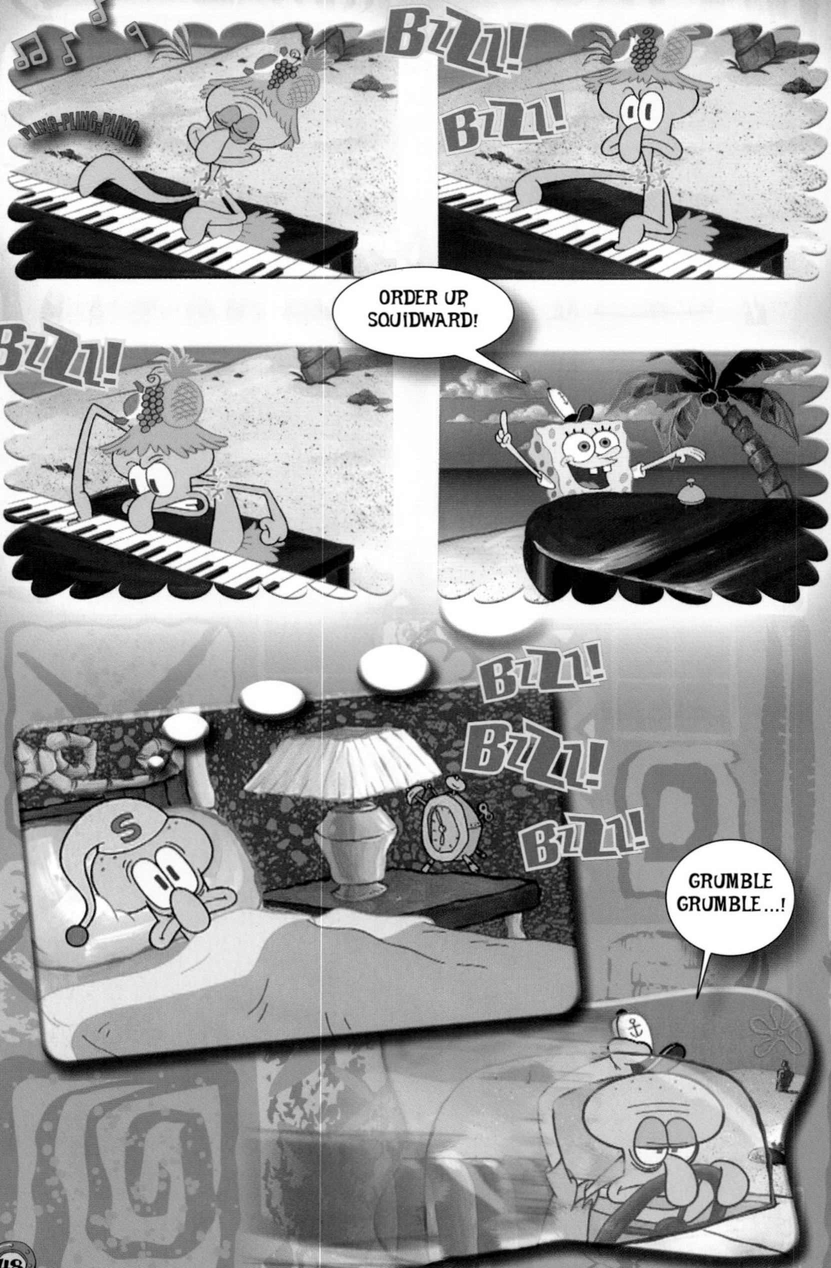

PLING-PLING-PLING
BZZZZ!
BZZZ!
BZZZZ!
ORDER UP, SQUIDWARD!
BZZZ!
BZZZZ!
BZZZ!
GRUMBLE GRUMBLE...!

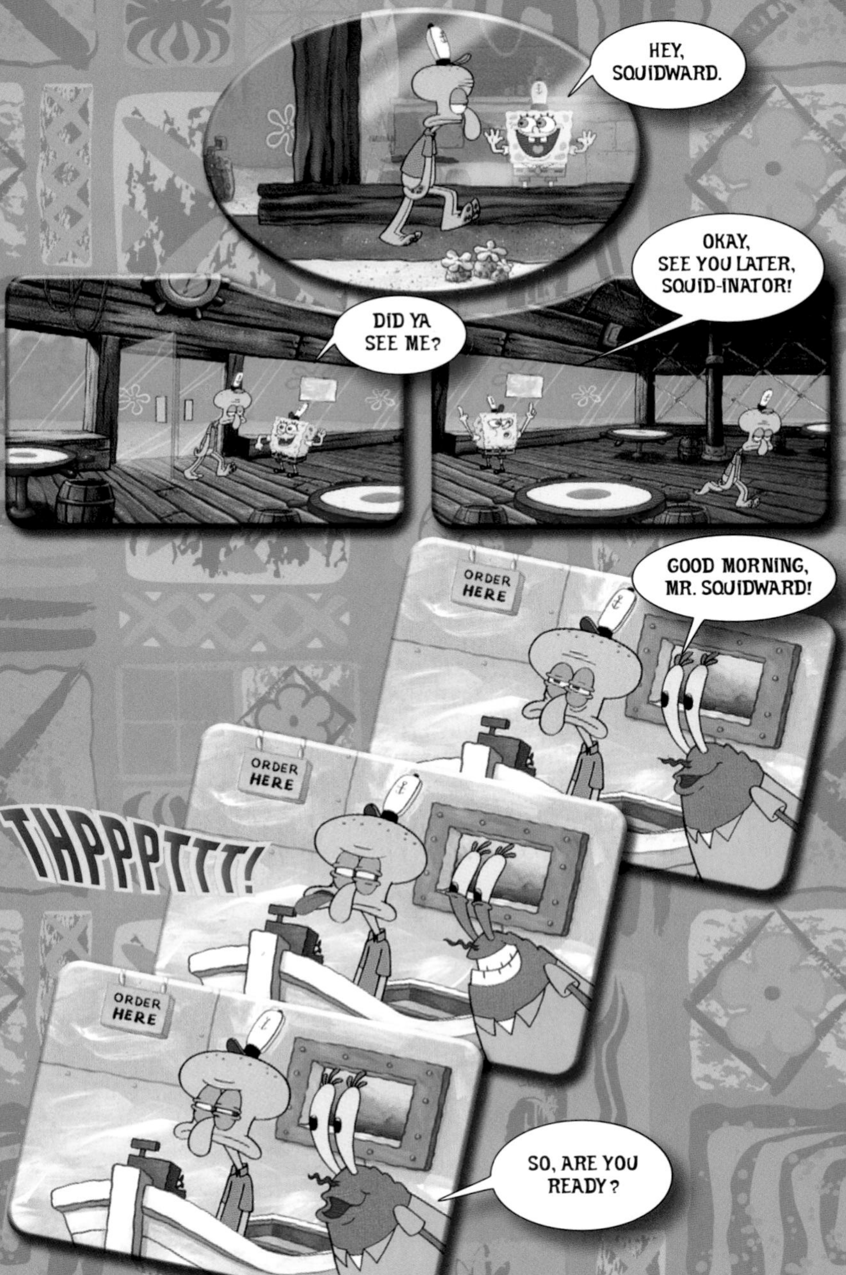
HEY, SQUIDWARD.
DID YA SEE ME?
OKAY, SEE YOU LATER, SQUID-INATOR!
GOOD MORNING, MR. SQUIDWARD!
THPPPTTT!
SO, ARE YOU READY?

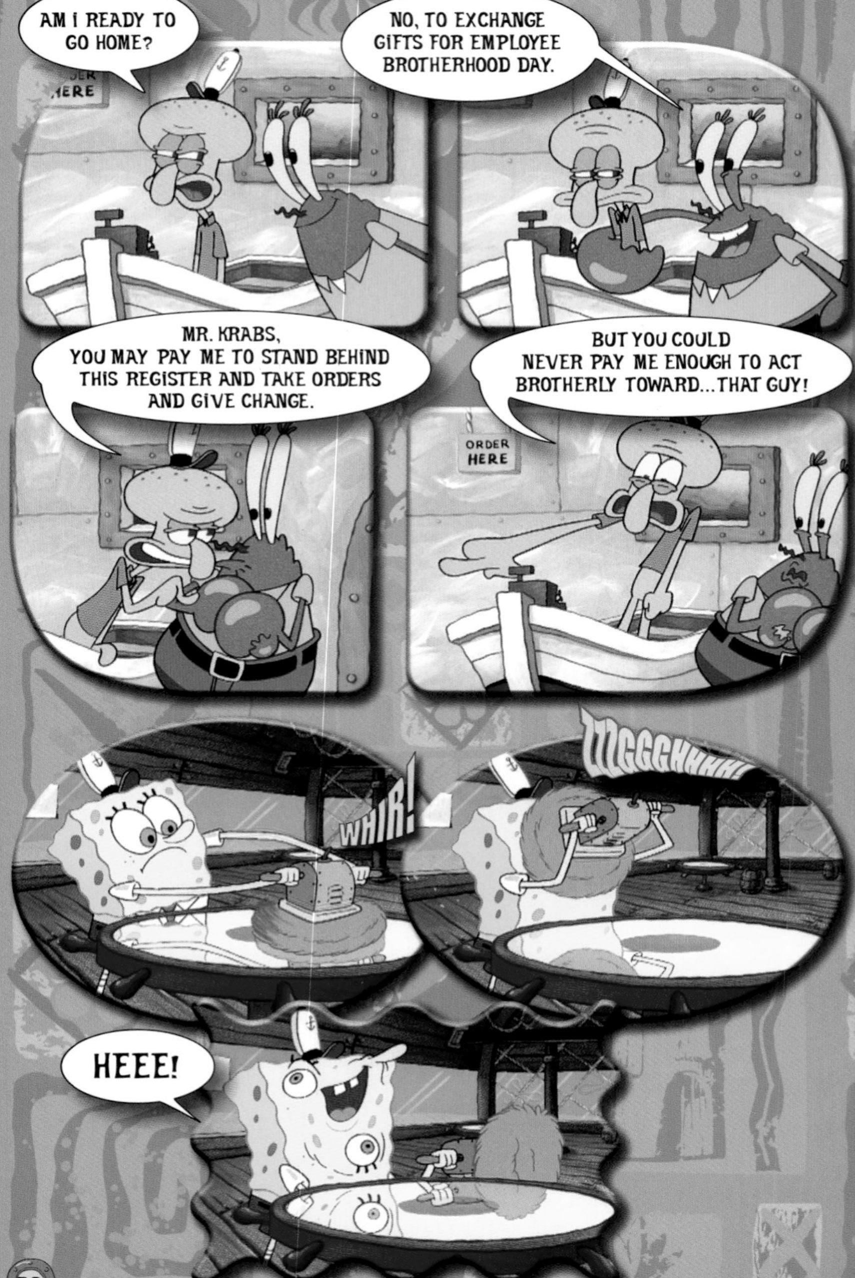
AM I READY TO GO HOME?
NO, TO EXCHANGE GIFTS FOR EMPLOYEE BROTHERHOOD DAY.
MR. KRABS, YOU MAY PAY ME TO STAND BEHIND THIS REGISTER AND TAKE ORDERS AND GIVE CHANGE.
BUT YOU COULD NEVER PAY ME ENOUGH TO ACT BROTHERLY TOWARD...THAT GUY!
ORDER HERE
WHIR!
HEEE!

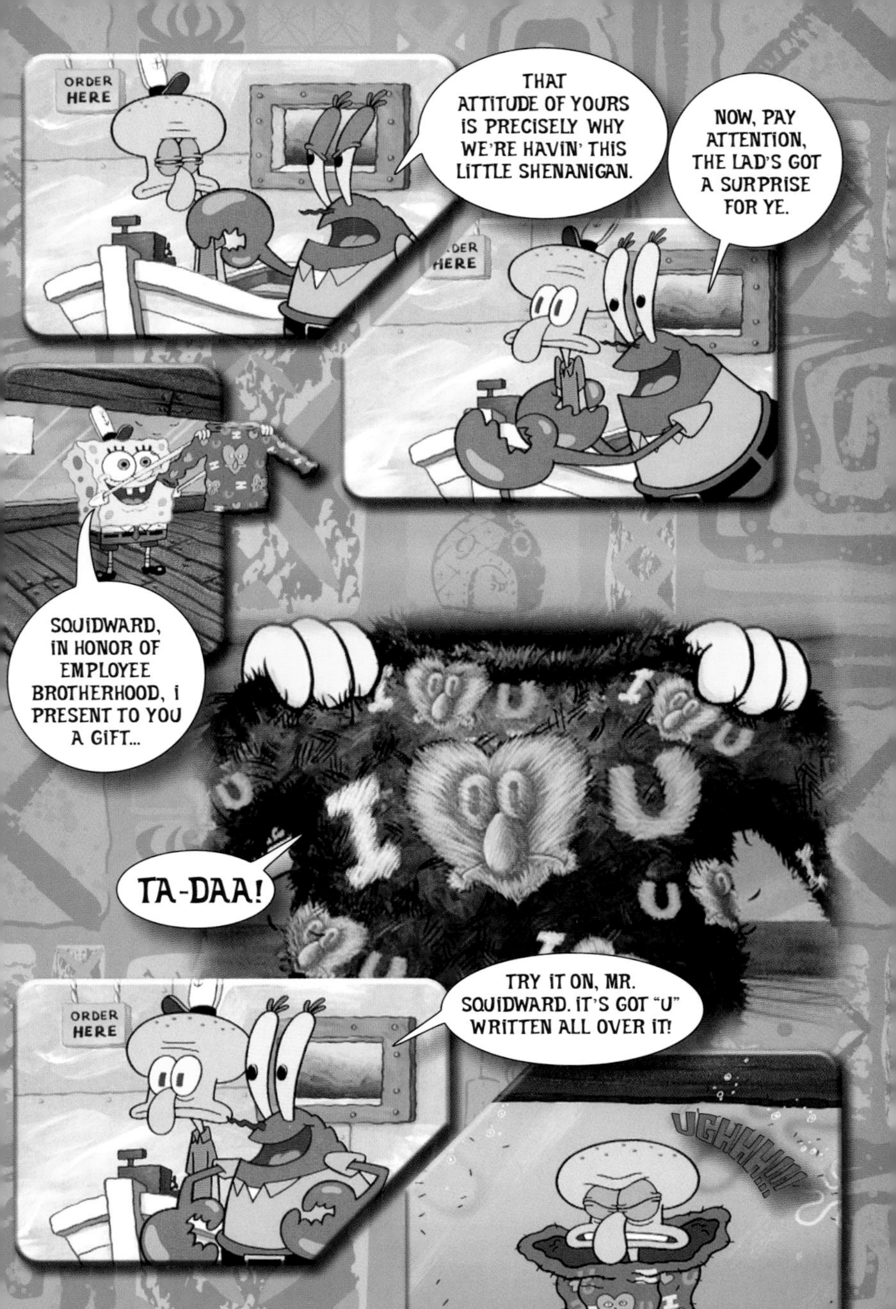
ORDER HERE
THAT ATTITUDE OF YOURS IS PRECISELY WHY WE'RE HAVIN' THIS LITTLE SHENANIGAN.
ORDER HERE
NOW, PAY ATTENTION, THE LAD'S GOT A SURPRISE FOR YE.
SQUIDWARD, IN HONOR OF EMPLOYEE BROTHERHOOD, I PRESENT TO YOU A GIFT...
TA-DAA!
ORDER HERE
TRY IT ON, MR. SQUIDWARD. IT'S GOT "U" WRITTEN ALL OVER IT!
UGHHHH...

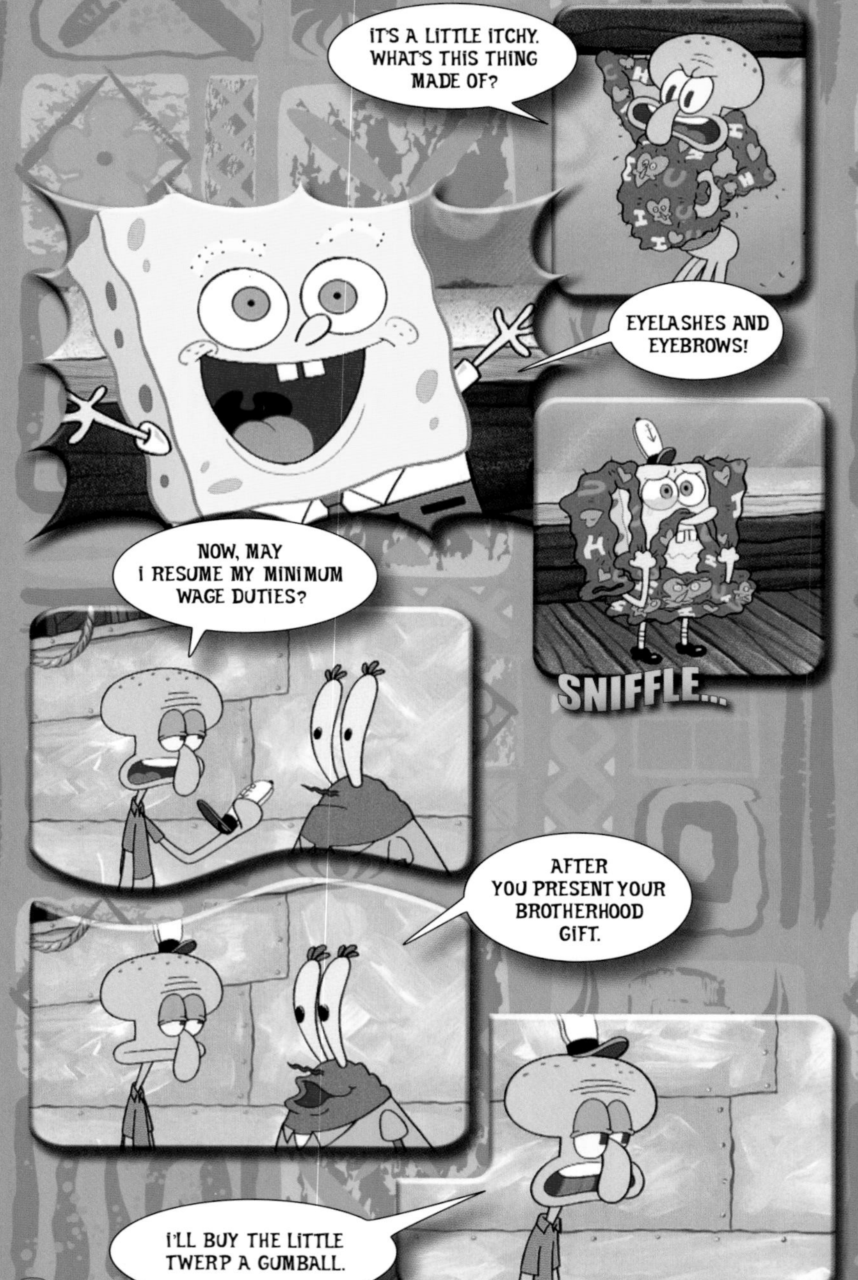
IT'S A LITTLE ITCHY. WHAT'S THIS THING MADE OF?
EYELASHES AND EYEBROWS!
SNIFFLE...
NOW, MAY I RESUME MY MINIMUM WAGE DUTIES?
AFTER YOU PRESENT YOUR BROTHERHOOD GIFT.
I'LL BUY THE LITTLE TWERP A GUMBALL.

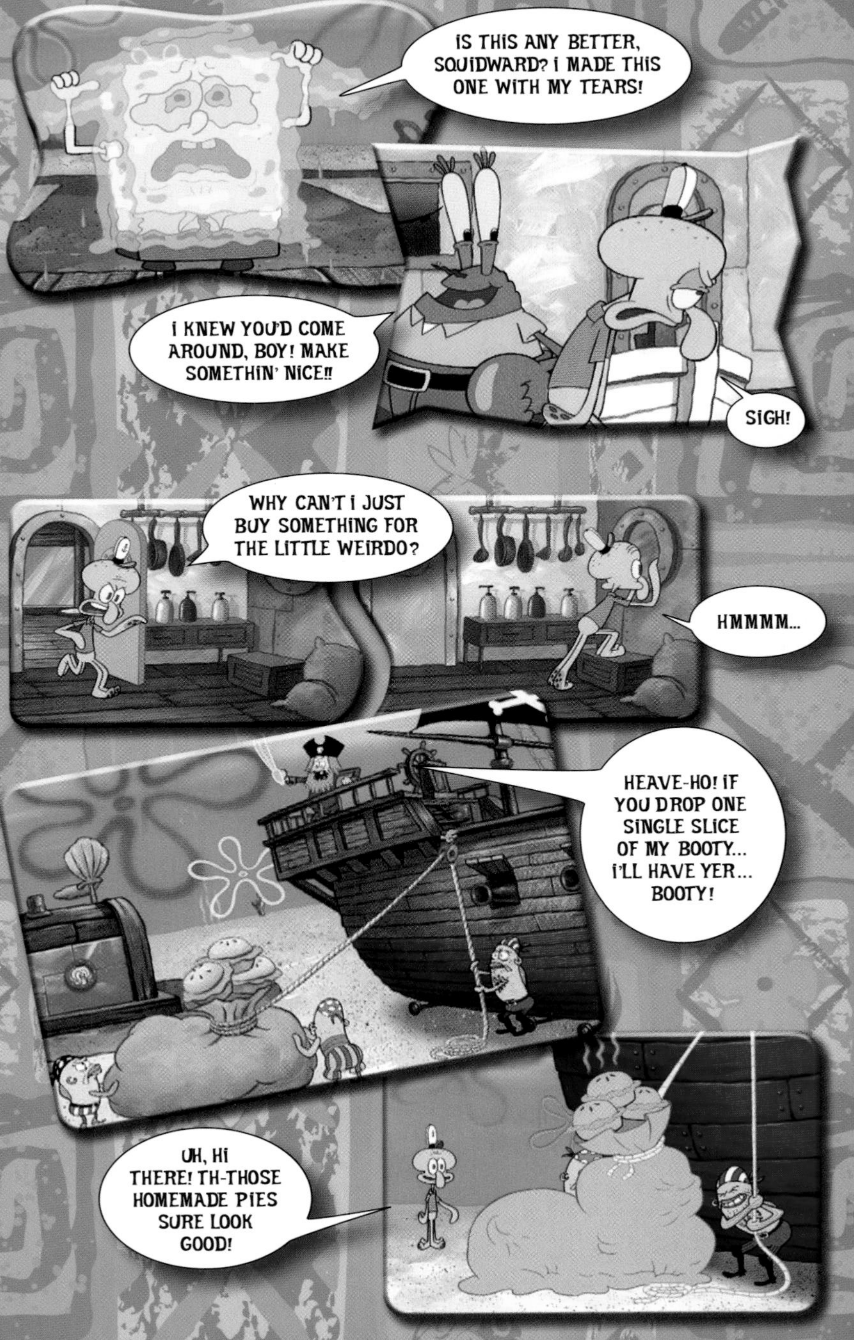
IS THIS ANY BETTER, SQUIDWARD? I MADE THIS ONE WITH MY TEARS!
I KNEW YOU'D COME AROUND, BOY! MAKE SOMETHIN' NICE!!
SIGH!
WHY CAN'T I JUST BUY SOMETHING FOR THE LITTLE WEIRDO?
HMMMM...
HEAVE-HO! IF YOU DROP ONE SINGLE SLICE OF MY BOOTY... I'LL HAVE YER... BOOTY!
UH, HI THERE! TH-THOSE HOMEMADE PIES SURE LOOK GOOD!

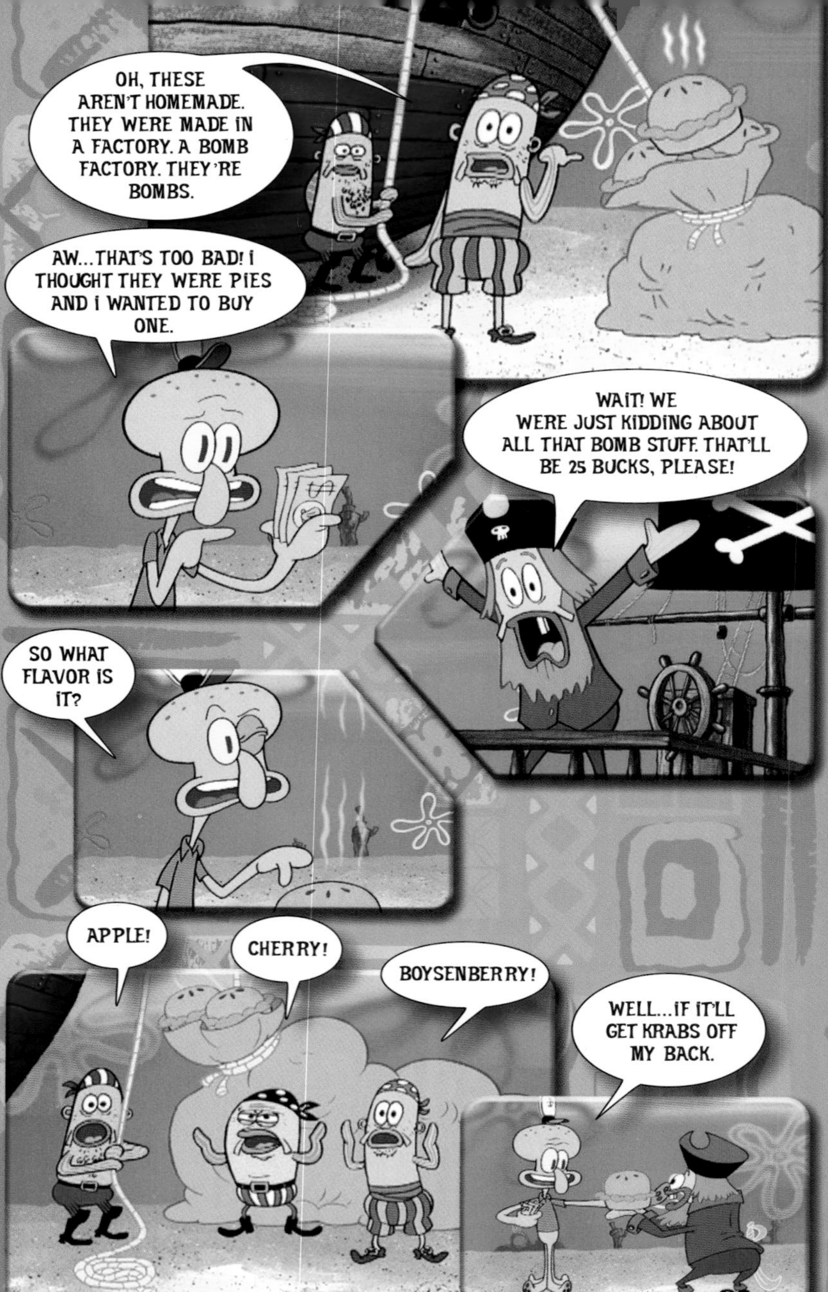
OH, THESE AREN'T HOMEMADE. THEY WERE MADE IN A FACTORY. A BOMB FACTORY. THEY'RE BOMBS.
AW...THAT'S TOO BAD! I THOUGHT THEY WERE PIES AND I WANTED TO BUY ONE.
WAIT! WE WERE JUST KIDDING ABOUT ALL THAT BOMB STUFF. THAT'LL BE 25 BUCKS, PLEASE!
SO WHAT FLAVOR IS IT?
APPLE!
CHERRY!
BOYSENBERRY!
WELL...IF IT'LL GET KRABS OFF MY BACK.

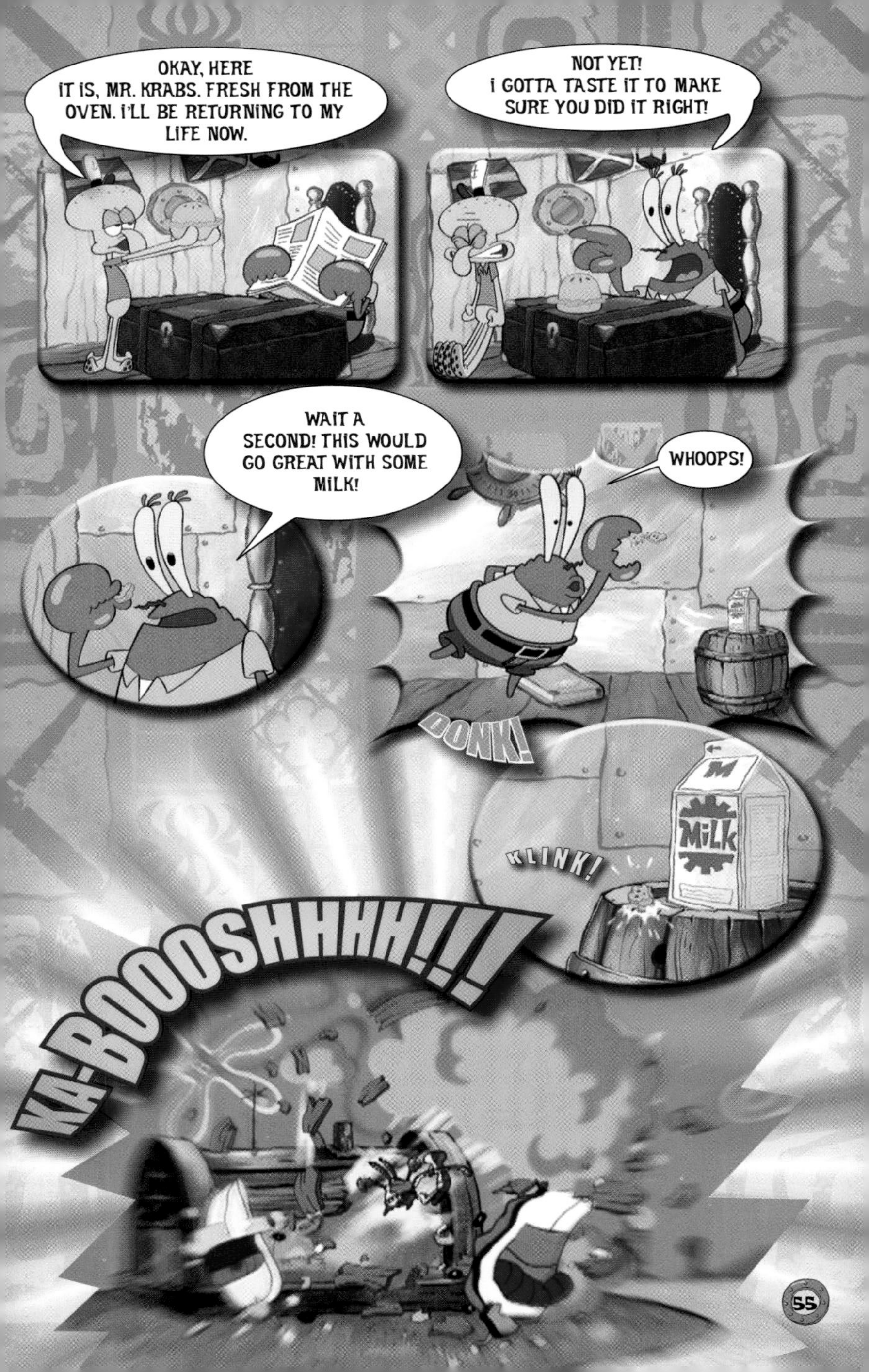
OKAY, HERE IT IS, MR. KRABS. FRESH FROM THE OVEN. I'LL BE RETURNING TO MY LIFE NOW.
NOT YET! I GOTTA TASTE IT TO MAKE SURE YOU DID IT RIGHT!
WAIT A SECOND! THIS WOULD GO GREAT WITH SOME MILK!
WHOOPS!
DONK!
MILK
KLINK!
KA-BOOOSHHHH!!!

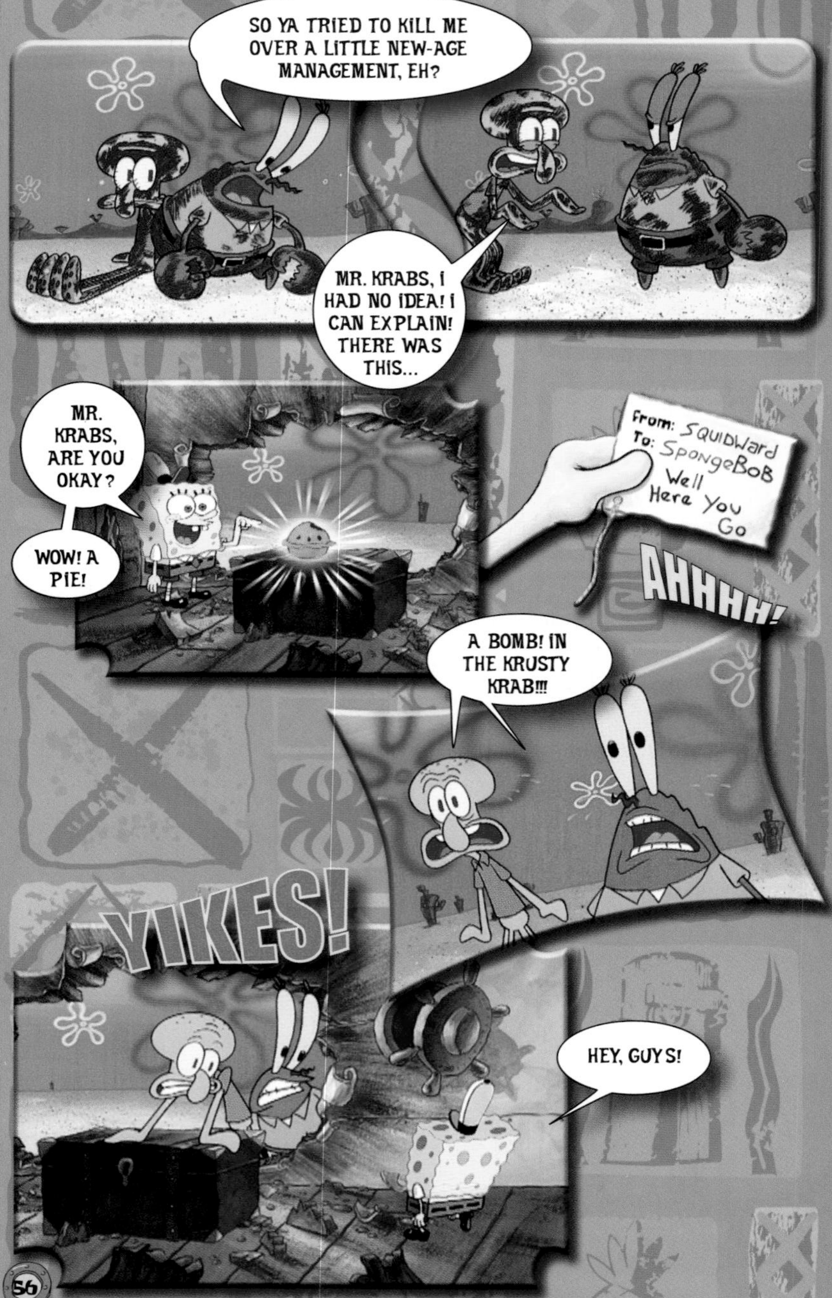
SO YA TRIED TO KILL ME OVER A LITTLE NEW-AGE MANAGEMENT, EH?
MR. KRABS, I HAD NO IDEA! I CAN EXPLAIN! THERE WAS THIS...
MR. KRABS, ARE YOU OKAY?
WOW! A PIE!
From: SQUIDWard To: SpongeBOB Well Here You Go
AHHHH!
A BOMB! IN THE KRUSTY KRAB!!!
YIKES!
HEY, GUYS!

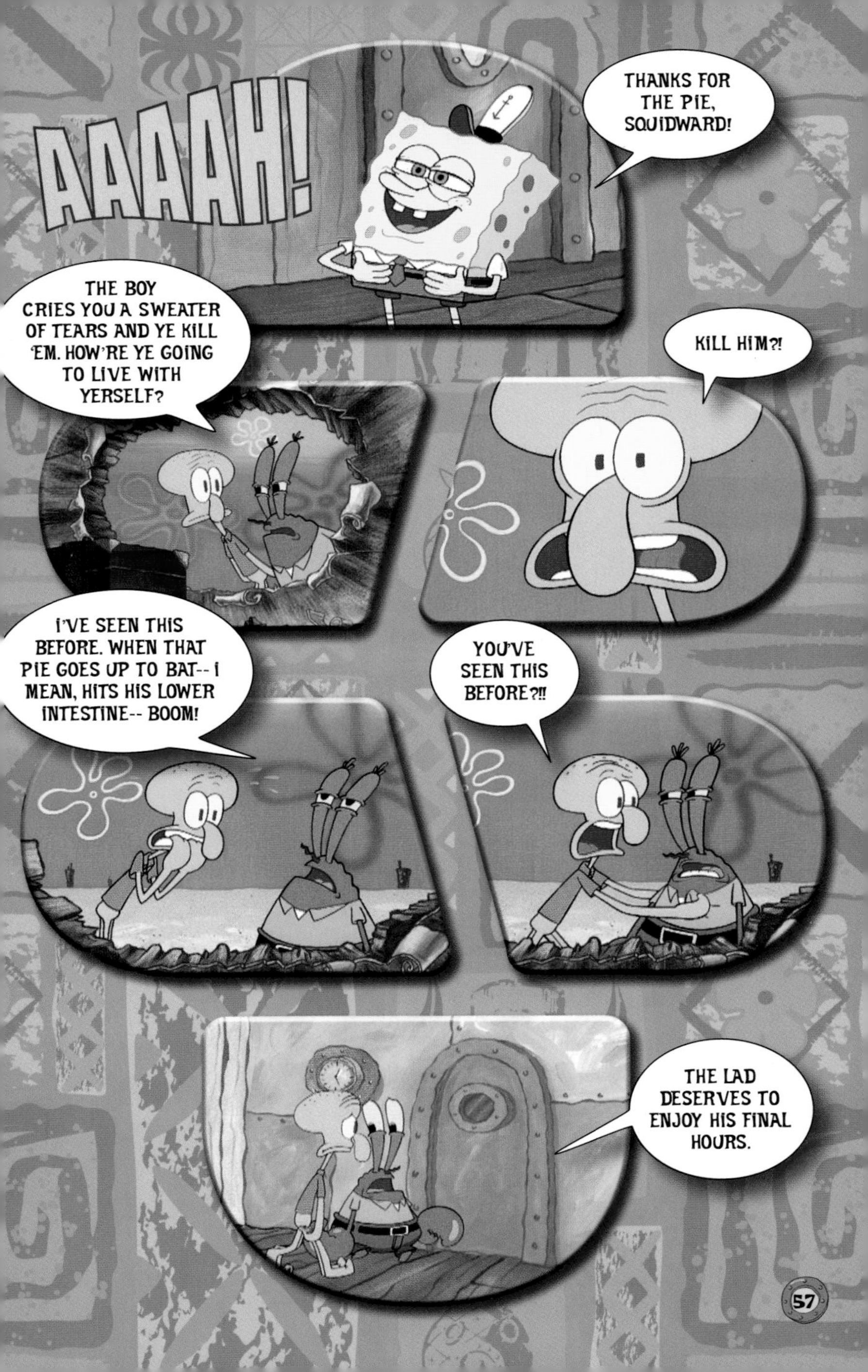
AAAAH!
THANKS FOR THE PIE, SQUIDWARD!
THE BOY CRIES YOU A SWEATER OF TEARS AND YE KILL 'EM. HOW'RE YE GOING TO LIVE WITH YERSELF?
KILL HIM?!
I'VE SEEN THIS BEFORE. WHEN THAT PIE GOES UP TO BAT-- I MEAN, HITS HIS LOWER INTESTINE-- BOOM!
YOU'VE SEEN THIS BEFORE?!!
THE LAD DESERVES TO ENJOY HIS FINAL HOURS.

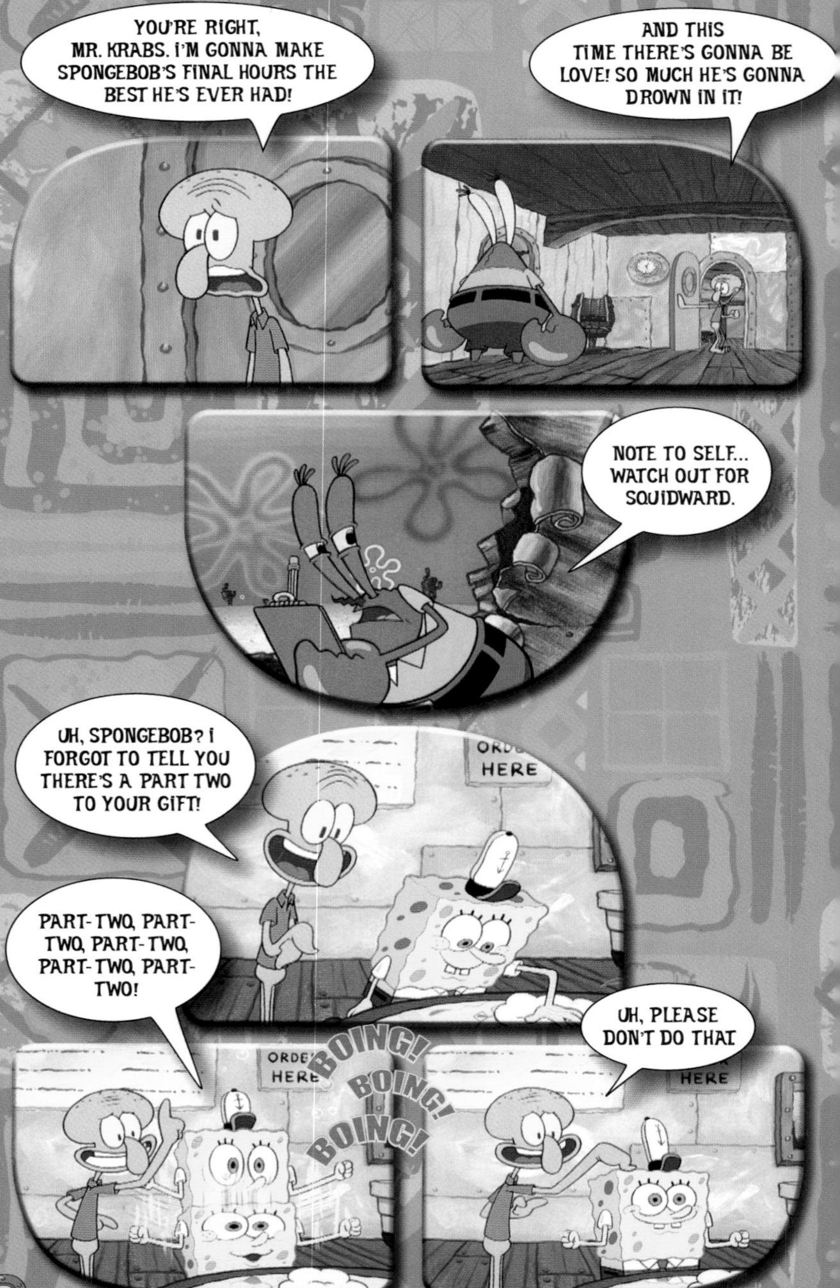
YOU'RE RIGHT, MR. KRABS. I'M GONNA MAKE SPONGEBOB'S FINAL HOURS THE BEST HE'S EVER HAD!
AND THIS TIME THERE'S GONNA BE LOVE! SO MUCH HE'S GONNA DROWN IN IT!
NOTE TO SELF... WATCH OUT FOR SQUIDWARD.
UH, SPONGEBOB? I FORGOT TO TELL YOU THERE'S A PART TWO TO YOUR GIFT!
ORDER HERE
PART-TWO, PART-TWO, PART-TWO, PART-TWO, PART-TWO!
BOING! BOING! BOING!
UH, PLEASE DON'T DO THAT
HERE

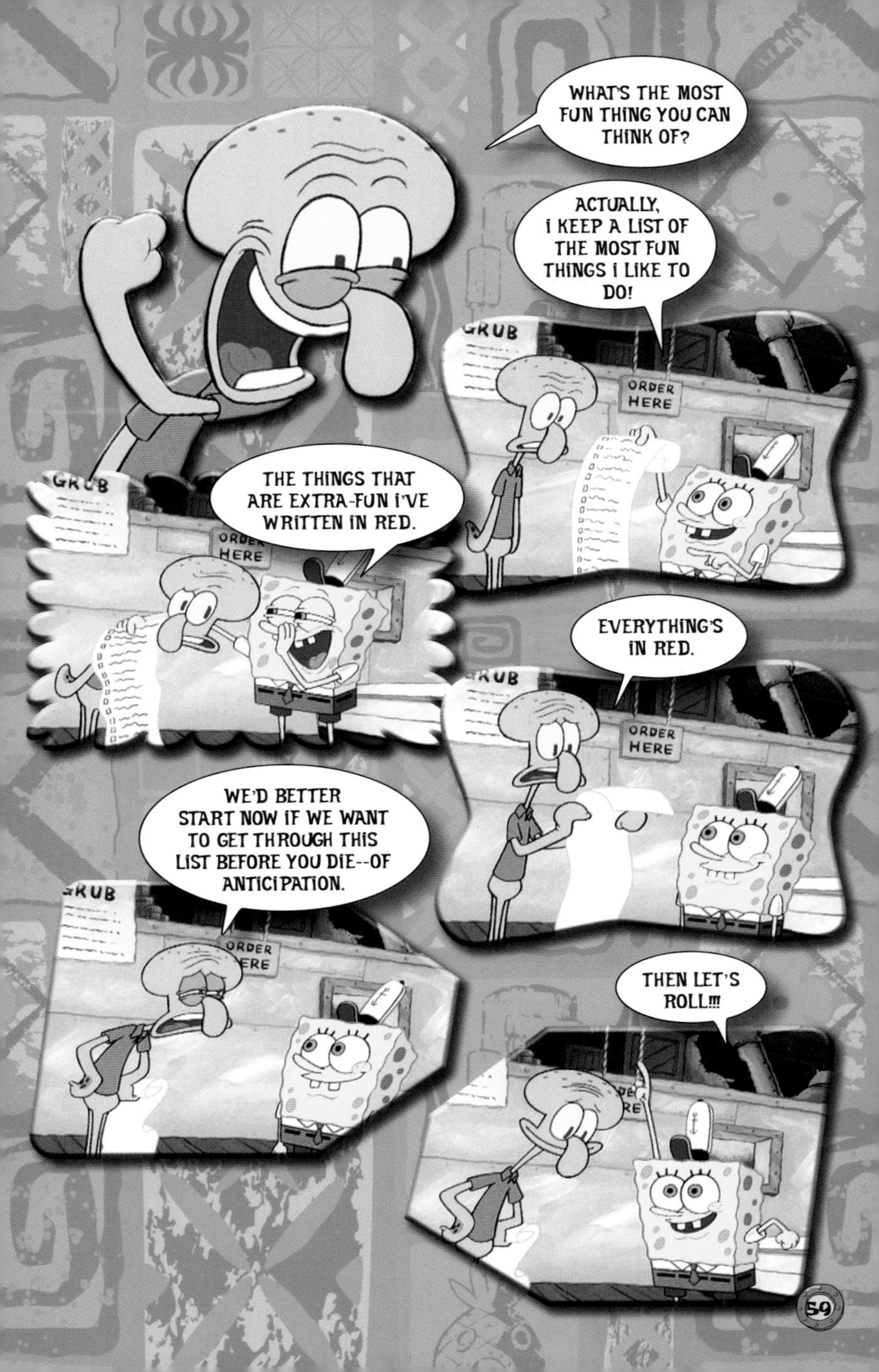
WHAT'S THE MOST FUN THING YOU CAN THINK OF?
ACTUALLY, I KEEP A LIST OF THE MOST FUN THINGS I LIKE TO DO!
GRUB
ORDER HERE
THE THINGS THAT ARE EXTRA-FUN I'VE WRITTEN IN RED.
EVERYTHING'S IN RED.
WE'D BETTER START NOW IF WE WANT TO GET THROUGH THIS LIST BEFORE YOU DIE--OF ANTICIPATION.
THEN LET'S ROLL!!!

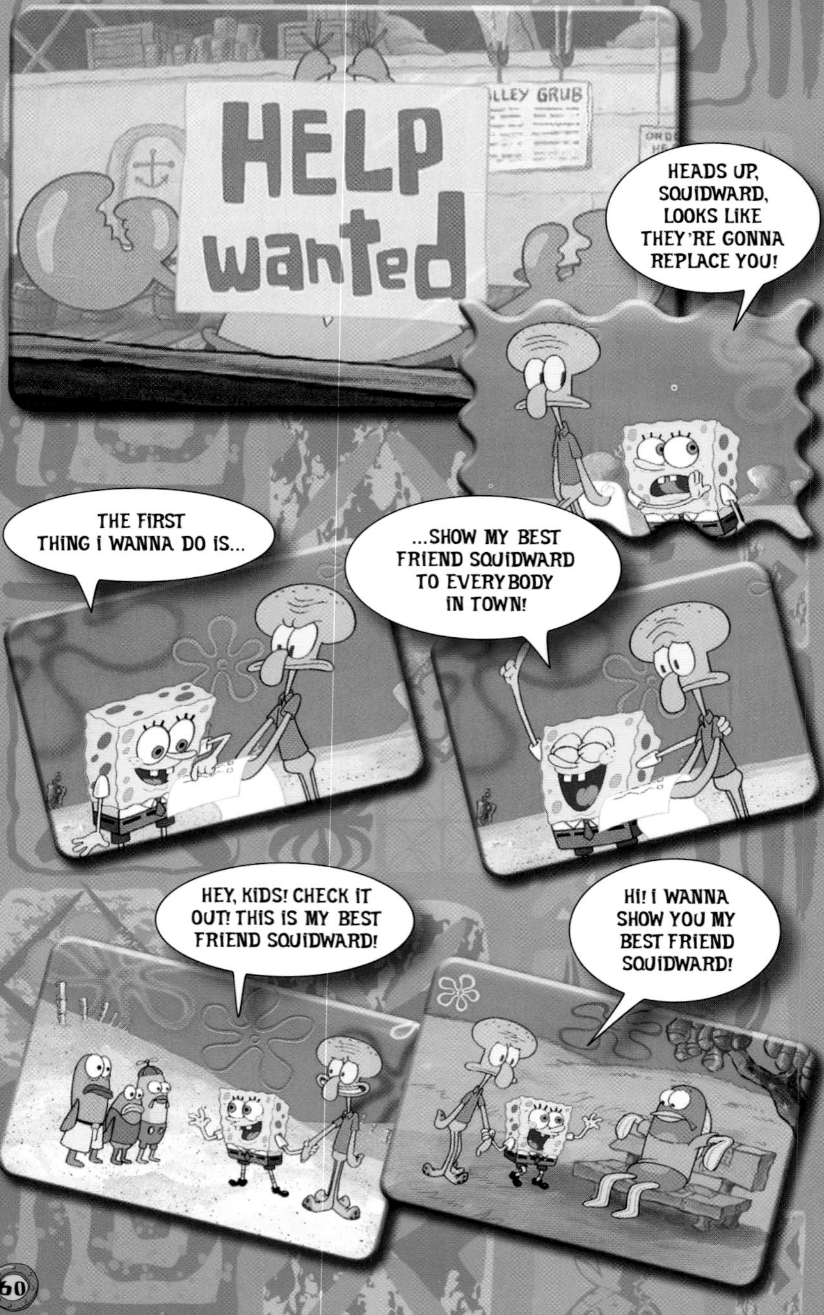
HELP
wanted
HEADS UP, SQUIDWARD, LOOKS LIKE THEY'RE GONNA REPLACE YOU!
THE FIRST THING I WANNA DO IS...
...SHOW MY BEST FRIEND SQUIDWARD TO EVERYBODY IN TOWN!
HEY, KIDS! CHECK IT OUT! THIS IS MY BEST FRIEND SQUIDWARD!
HI! I WANNA SHOW YOU MY BEST FRIEND SQUIDWARD!

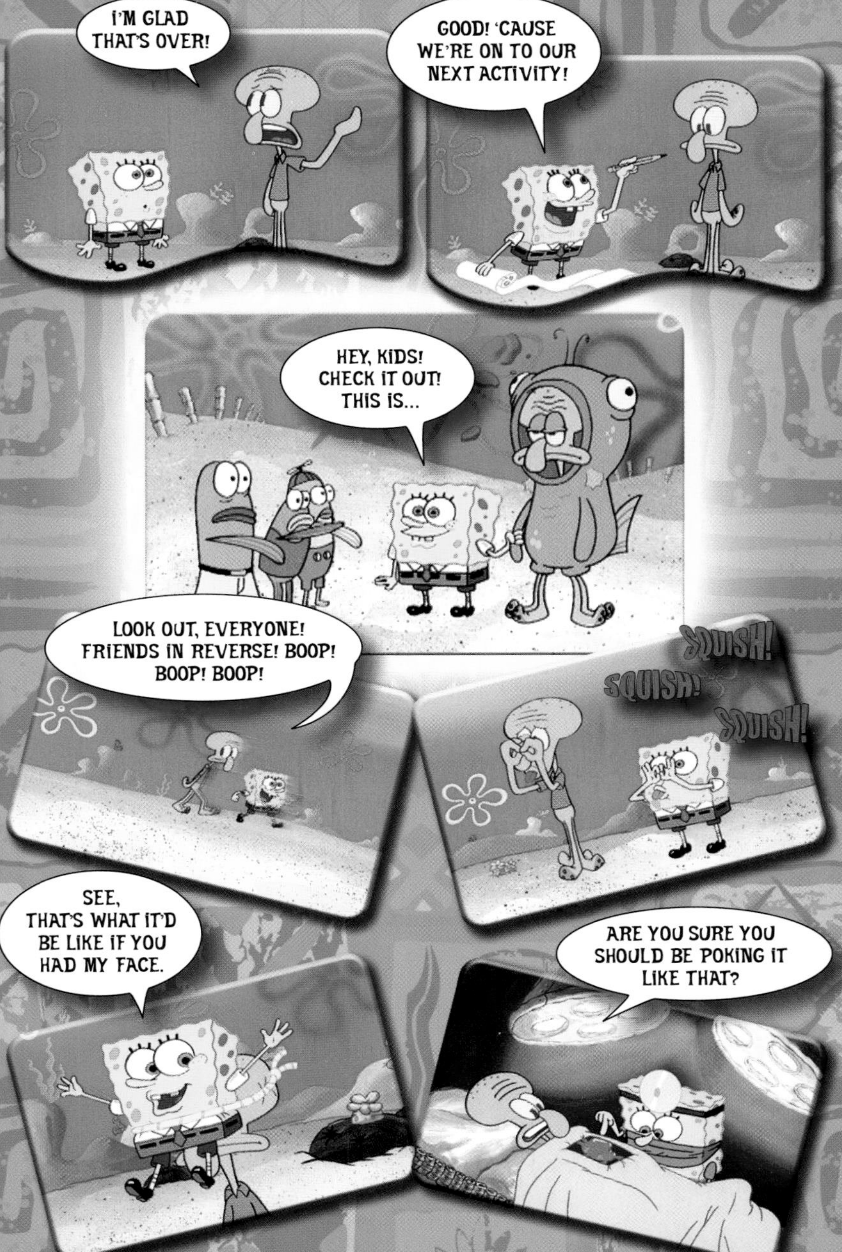
I'M GLAD THAT'S OVER!
GOOD! 'CAUSE WE'RE ON TO OUR NEXT ACTIVITY!
HEY, KIDS! CHECK IT OUT! THIS IS...
LOOK OUT, EVERYONE! FRIENDS IN REVERSE! BOOP! BOOP! BOOP!
SQUISH!
SQUISH!
SQUISH!
SEE, THAT'S WHAT IT'D BE LIKE IF YOU HAD MY FACE.
ARE YOU SURE YOU SHOULD BE POKING IT LIKE THAT?

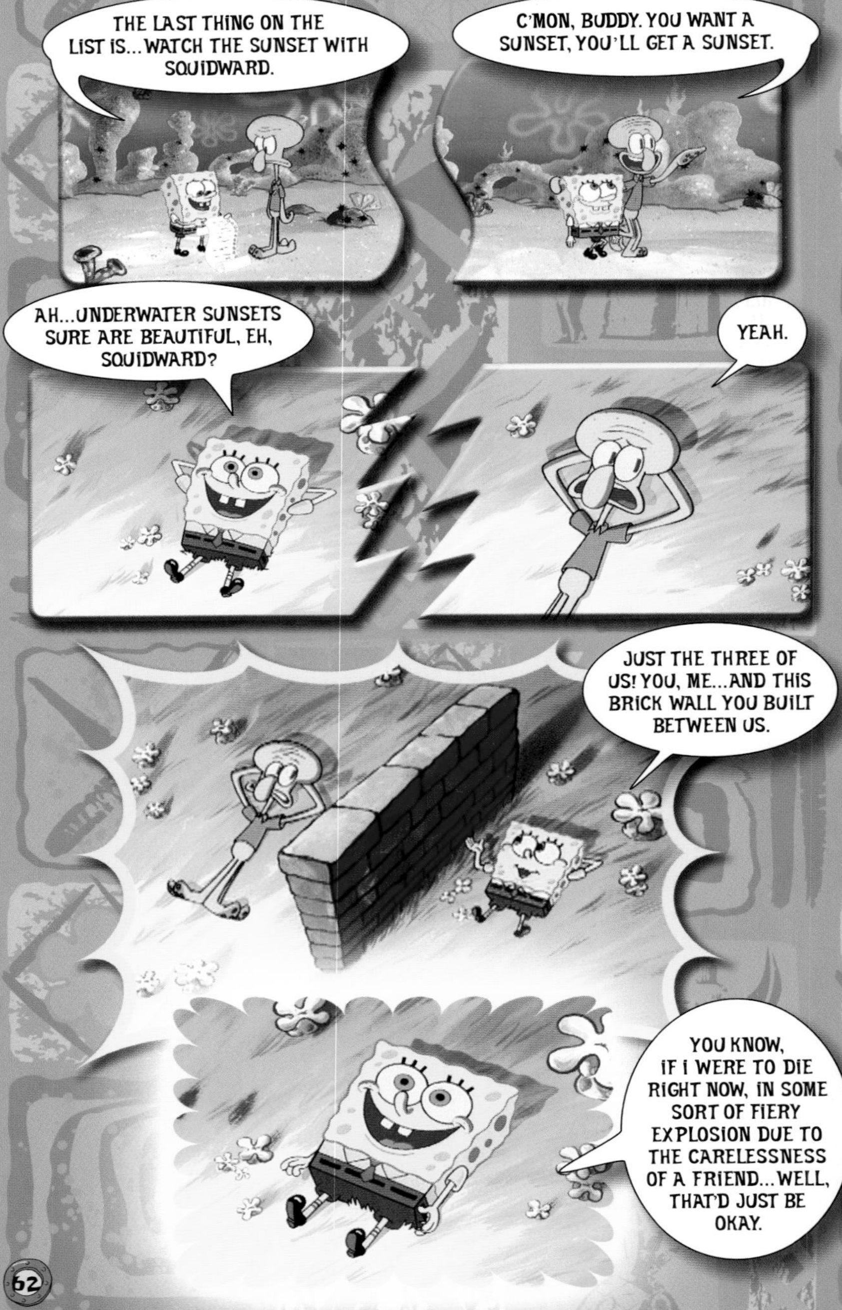
THE LAST THING ON THE LIST IS...WATCH THE SUNSET WITH SQUIDWARD.
C'MON, BUDDY. YOU WANT A SUNSET, YOU'LL GET A SUNSET.
AH...UNDERWATER SUNSETS SURE ARE BEAUTIFUL, EH, SQUIDWARD?
YEAH.
JUST THE THREE OF US! YOU, ME...AND THIS BRICK WALL YOU BUILT BETWEEN US.
YOU KNOW, IF I WERE TO DIE RIGHT NOW, IN SOME SORT OF FIERY EXPLOSION DUE TO THE CARELESSNESS OF A FRIEND...WELL, THAT'D JUST BE OKAY.

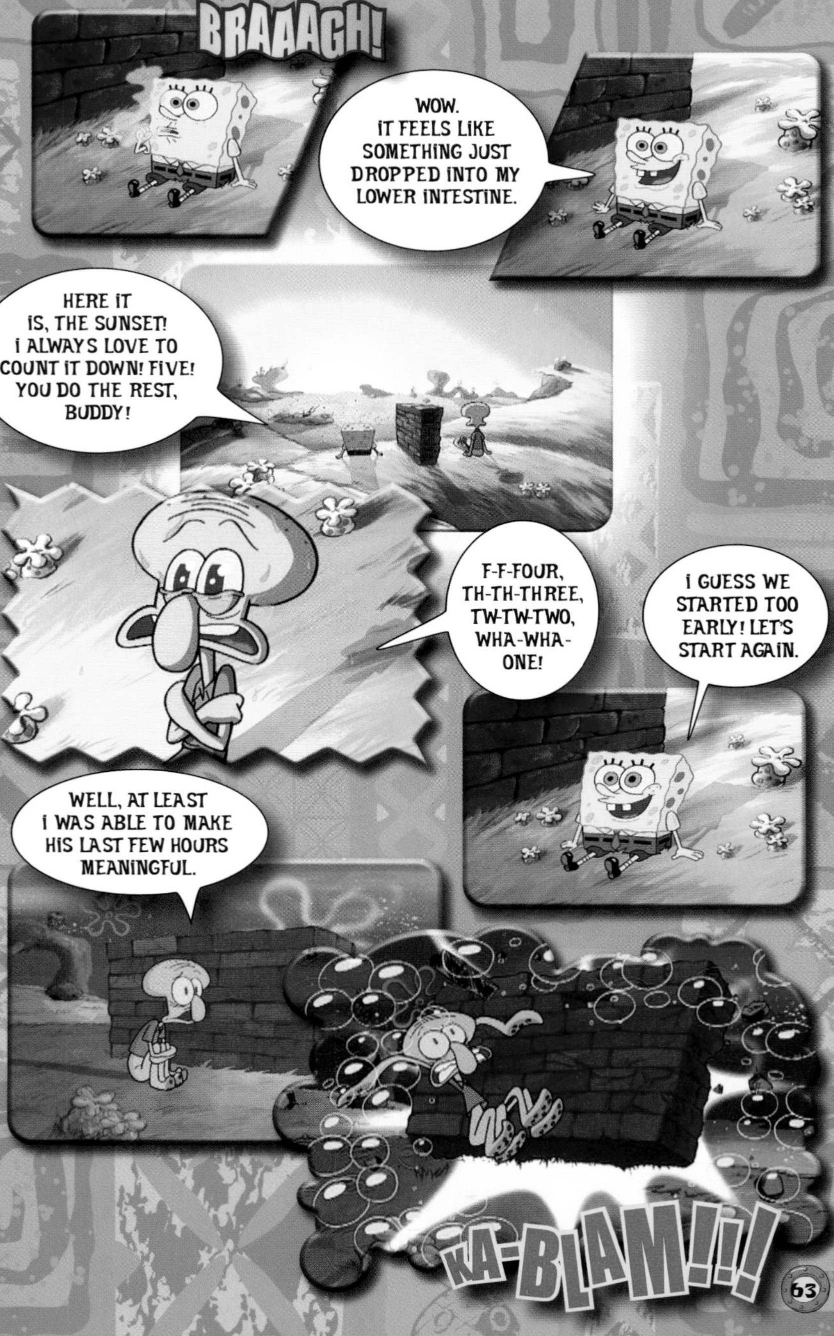
BRAAAGH!
WOW. IT FEELS LIKE SOMETHING JUST DROPPED INTO MY LOWER INTESTINE.
HERE IT IS, THE SUNSET! I ALWAYS LOVE TO COUNT IT DOWN! FIVE! YOU DO THE REST, BUDDY!
F-F-FOUR, TH-TH-THREE, TW-TW-TWO, WHA-WHA-ONE!
I GUESS WE STARTED TOO EARLY! LET'S START AGAIN.
WELL, AT LEAST I WAS ABLE TO MAKE HIS LAST FEW HOURS MEANINGFUL.
KA-BLAM!!!!

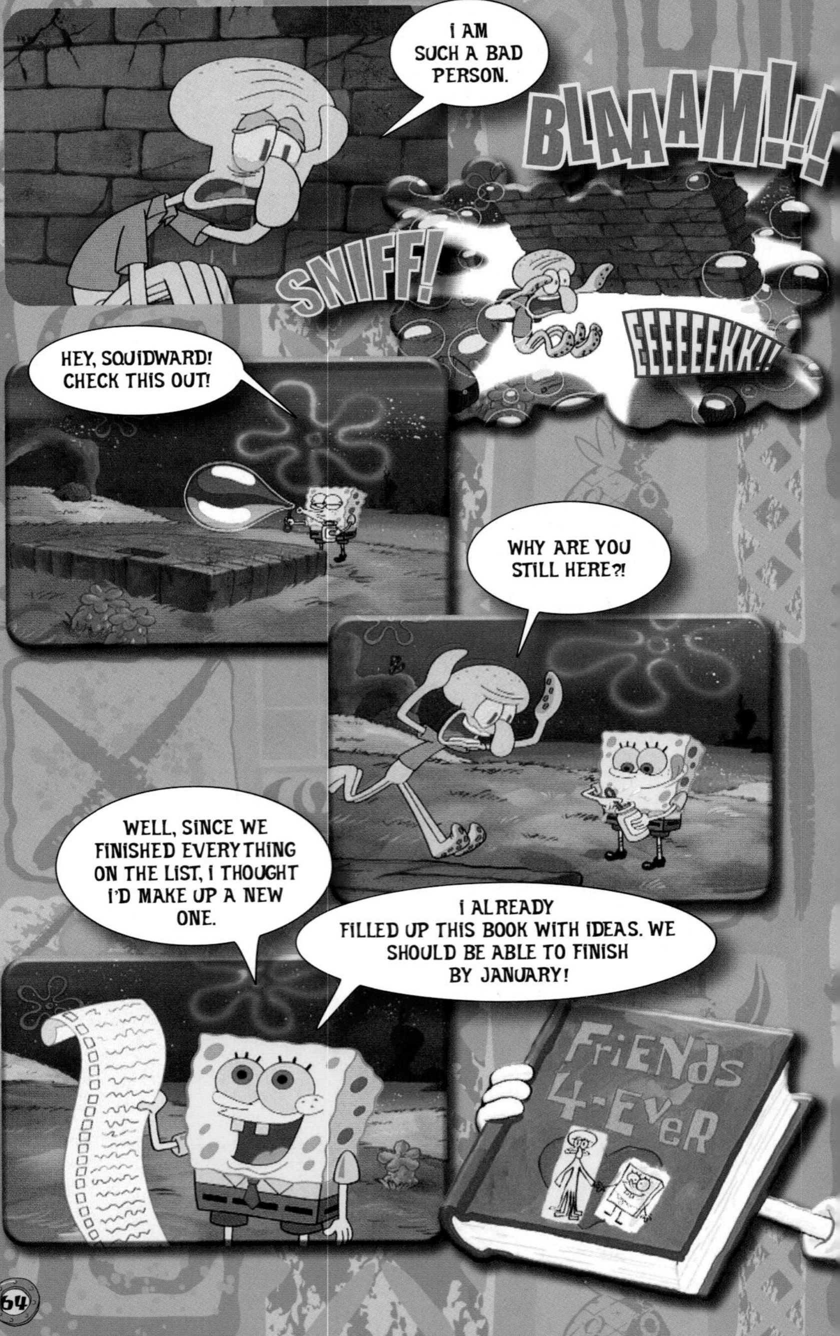
I AM SUCH A BAD PERSON.
SNIFF!
BLAAAM!!!
EEEEEEKK!!
HEY, SQUIDWARD! CHECK THIS OUT!
WHY ARE YOU STILL HERE?!
WELL, SINCE WE FINISHED EVERYTHING ON THE LIST, I THOUGHT I'D MAKE UP A NEW ONE.
I ALREADY FILLED UP THIS BOOK WITH IDEAS. WE SHOULD BE ABLE TO FINISH BY JANUARY!
FRIENDS 4-EVER

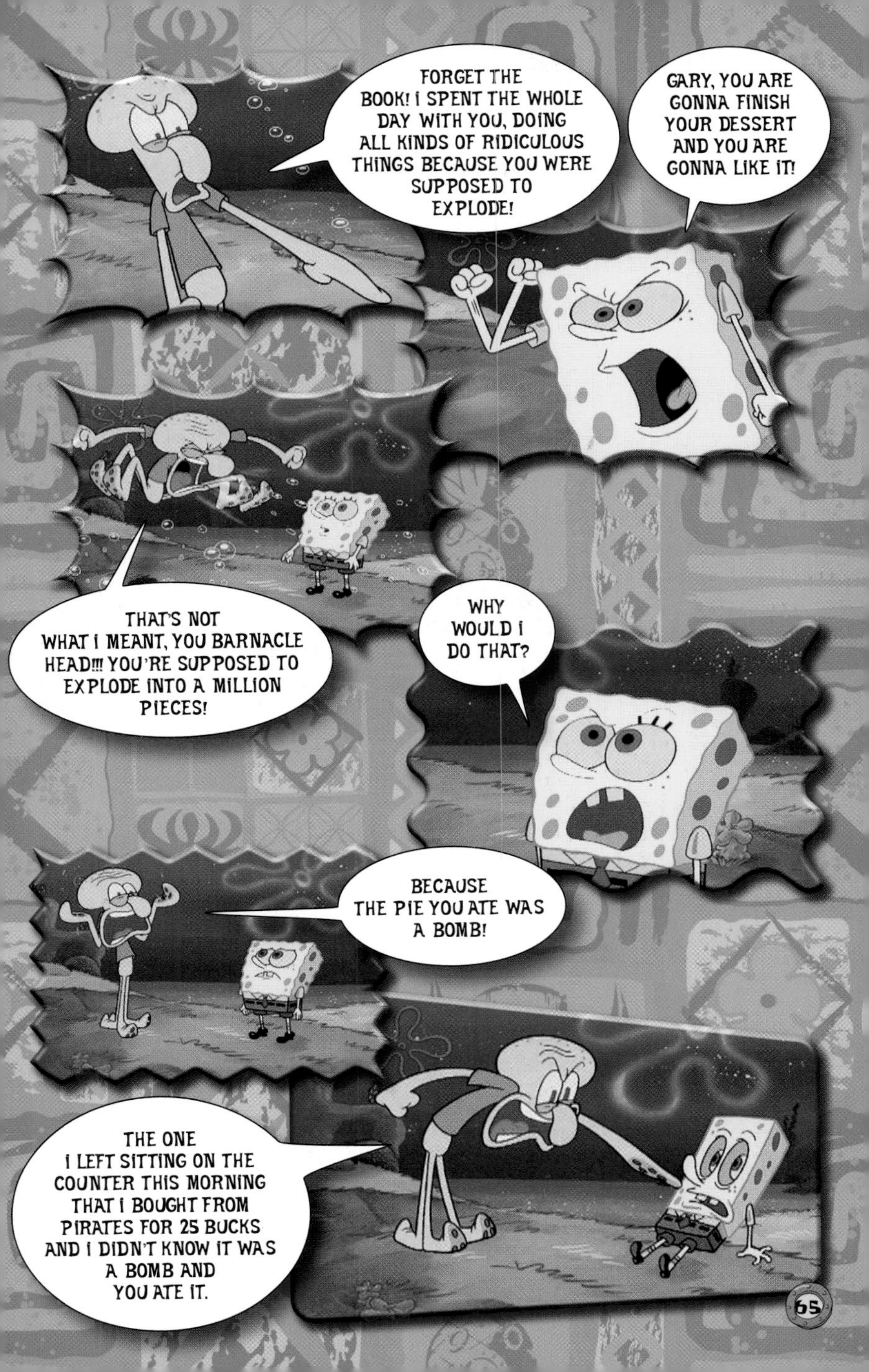
FORGET THE BOOK! I SPENT THE WHOLE DAY WITH YOU, DOING ALL KINDS OF RIDICULOUS THINGS BECAUSE YOU WERE SUPPOSED TO EXPLODE!
GARY, YOU ARE GONNA FINISH YOUR DESSERT AND YOU ARE GONNA LIKE IT!
THAT'S NOT WHAT I MEANT, YOU BARNACLE HEAD!!! YOU'RE SUPPOSED TO EXPLODE INTO A MILLION PIECES!
WHY WOULD I DO THAT?
BECAUSE THE PIE YOU ATE WAS A BOMB!
THE ONE I LEFT SITTING ON THE COUNTER THIS MORNING THAT I BOUGHT FROM PIRATES FOR 25 BUCKS AND I DIDN'T KNOW IT WAS A BOMB AND YOU ATE IT.

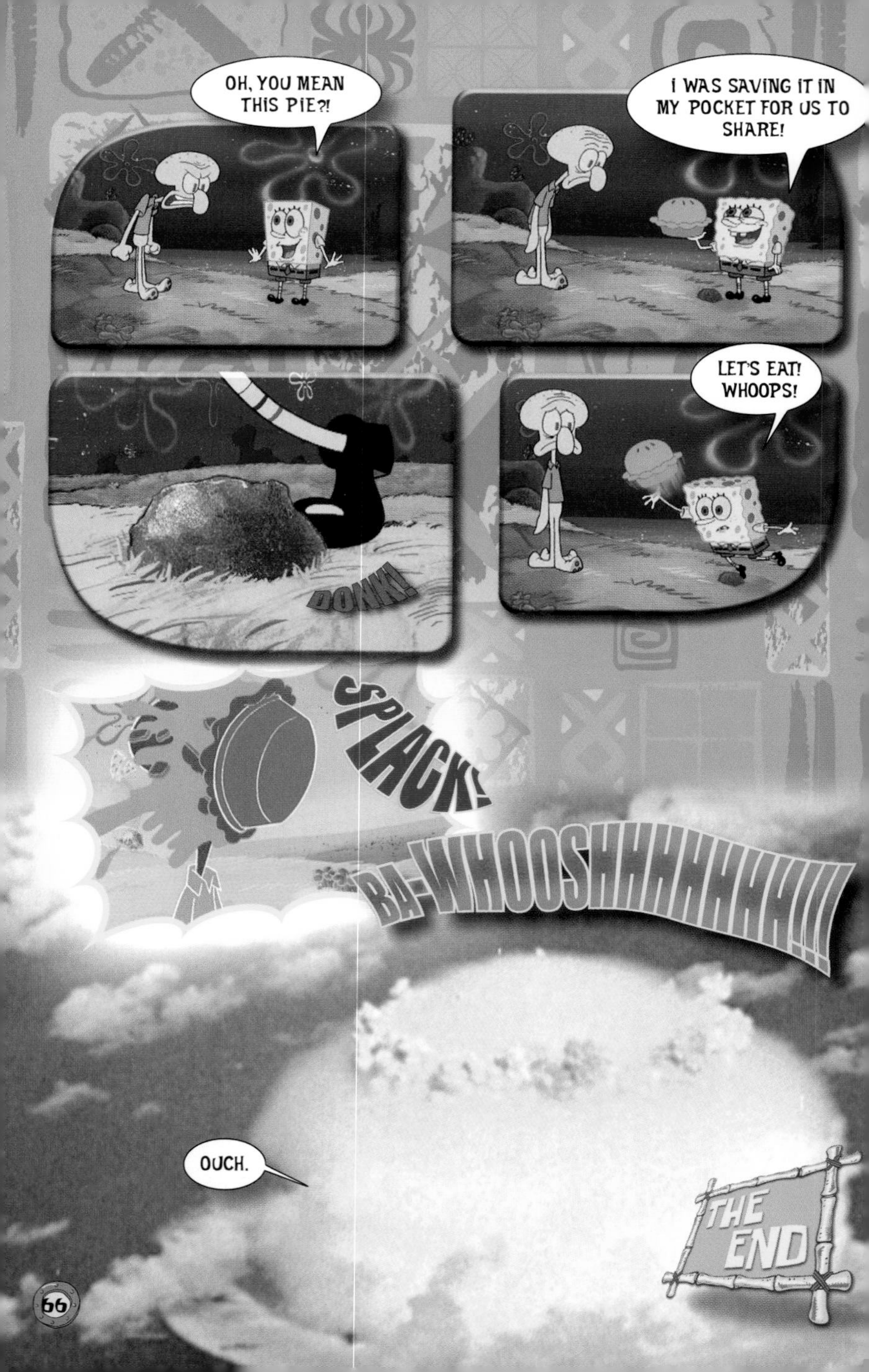
OH, YOU MEAN THIS PIE?!
I WAS SAVING IT IN MY POCKET FOR US TO SHARE!
DONK!
LET'S EAT! WHOOPS!
SPLACK!
BA-WHOOSHHHHHHHH!!!
OUCH.
THE END

SpongeBob SquarePants

Clams

By Jay Lender, Sam Henderson and Mark O'Hare

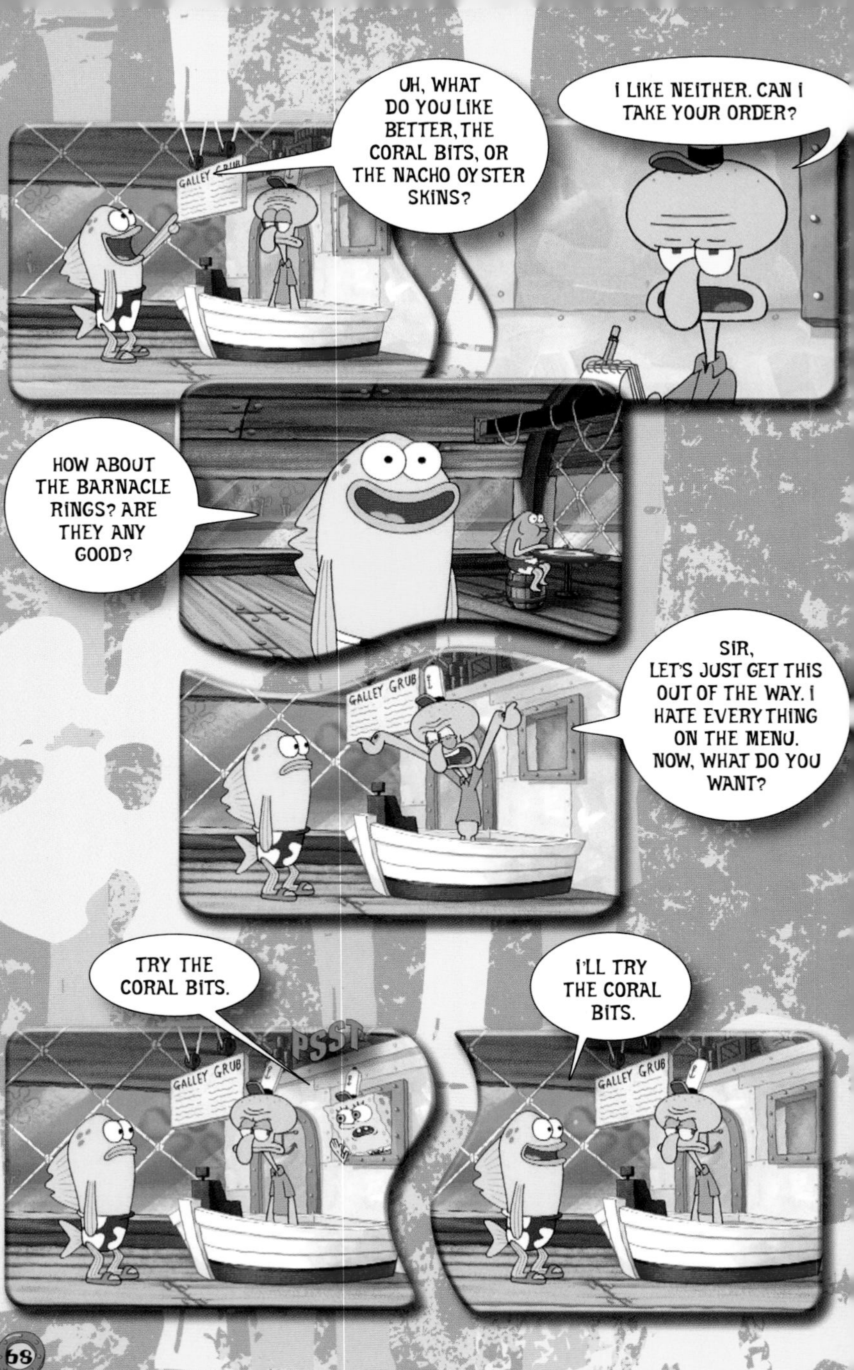
UH, WHAT DO YOU LIKE BETTER, THE CORAL BITS, OR THE NACHO OYSTER SKINS?
GALLEY GRUB
I LIKE NEITHER. CAN I TAKE YOUR ORDER?
HOW ABOUT THE BARNACLE RINGS? ARE THEY ANY GOOD?
GALLEY GRUB
SIR, LET'S JUST GET THIS OUT OF THE WAY. I HATE EVERYTHING ON THE MENU. NOW, WHAT DO YOU WANT?
TRY THE CORAL BITS.
PSST
GALLEY GRUB
I'LL TRY THE CORAL BITS.
GALLEY GRUB

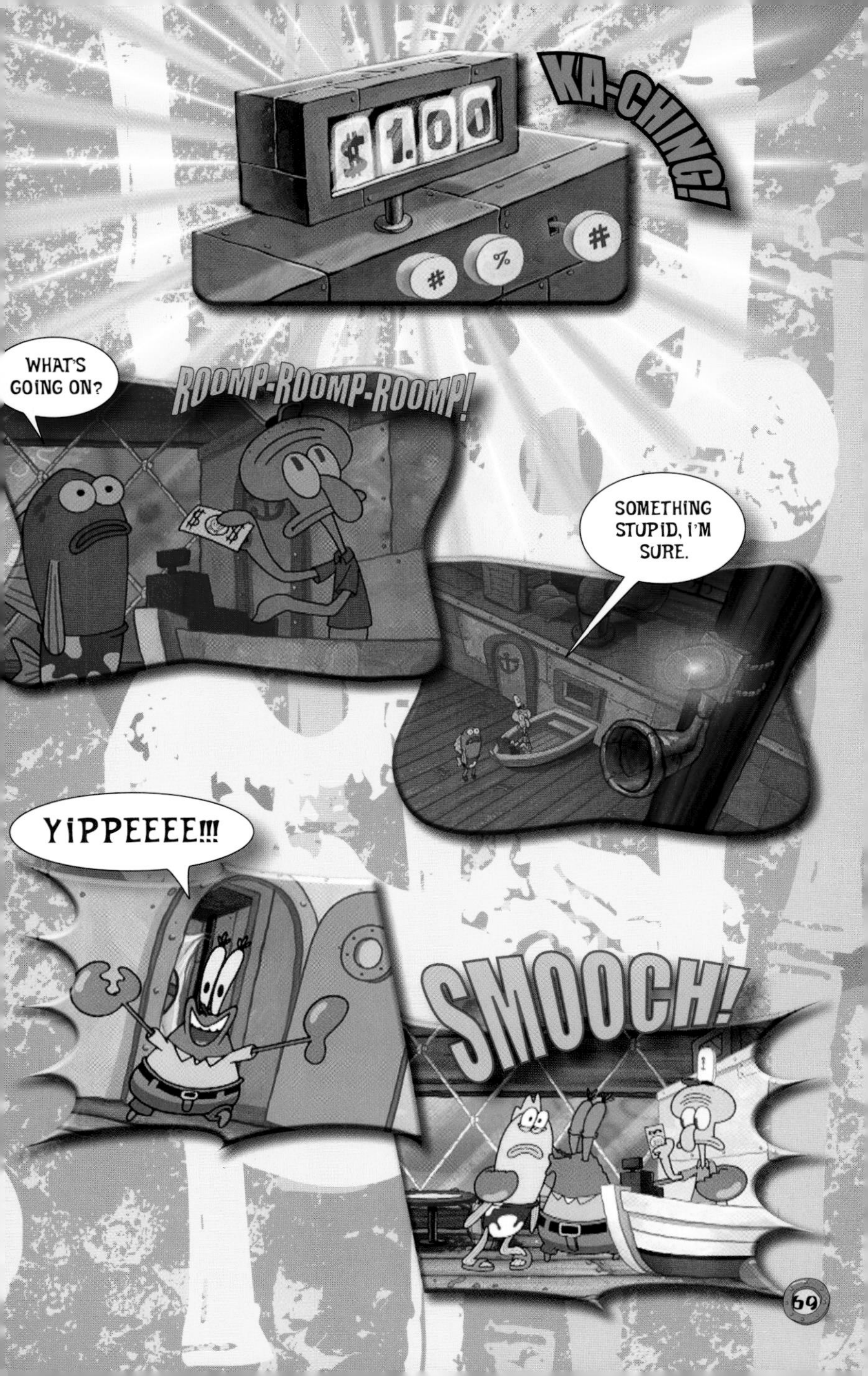
$1.00
KA-CHING!
%
#
WHAT'S GOING ON?
ROOMP-ROOMP-ROOMP!
SOMETHING STUPID, I'M SURE.
YIPPEEEE!!!
SMOOCH!

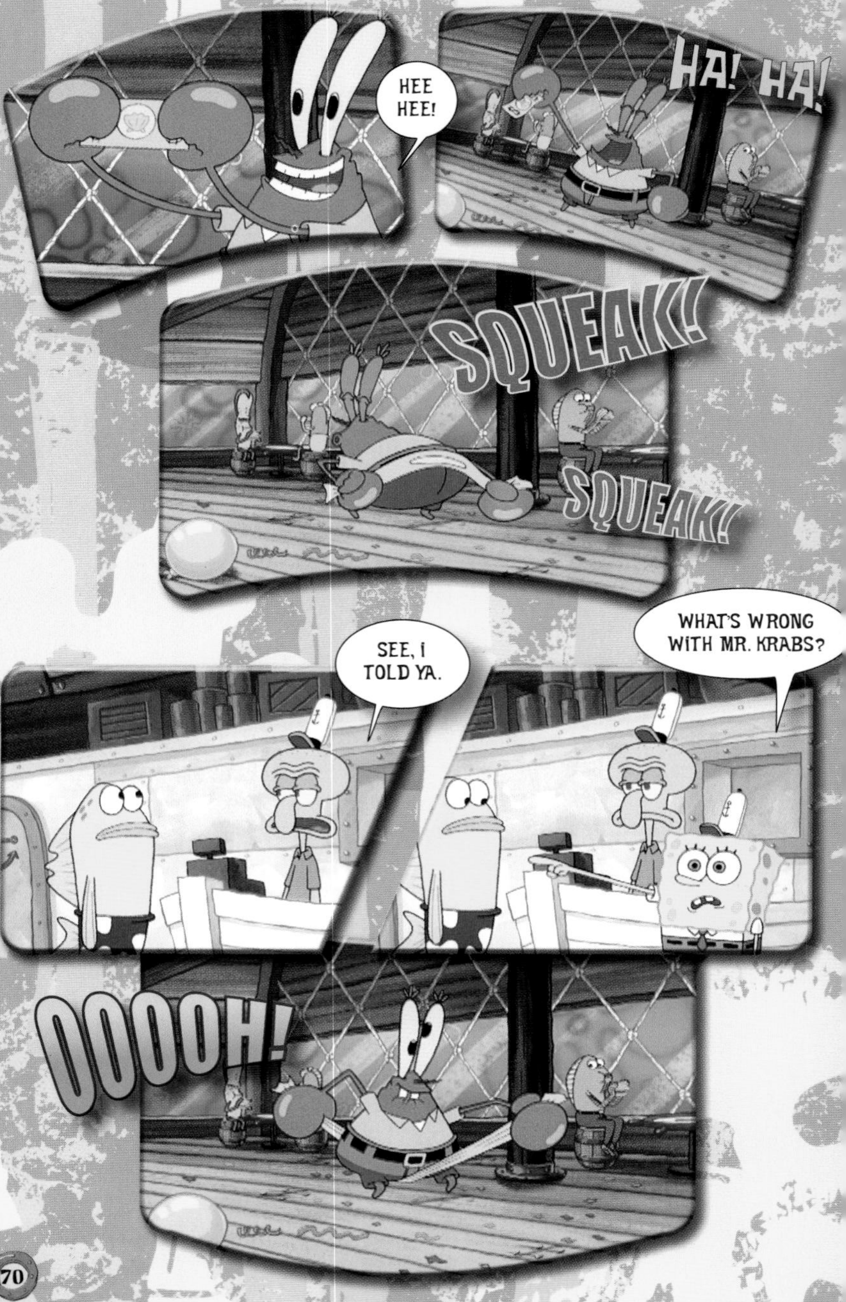
HEE HEE!
HA! HA!
SQUEAK!
SQUEAK!
SEE, I TOLD YA.
WHAT'S WRONG WITH MR. KRABS?
OOOOH!

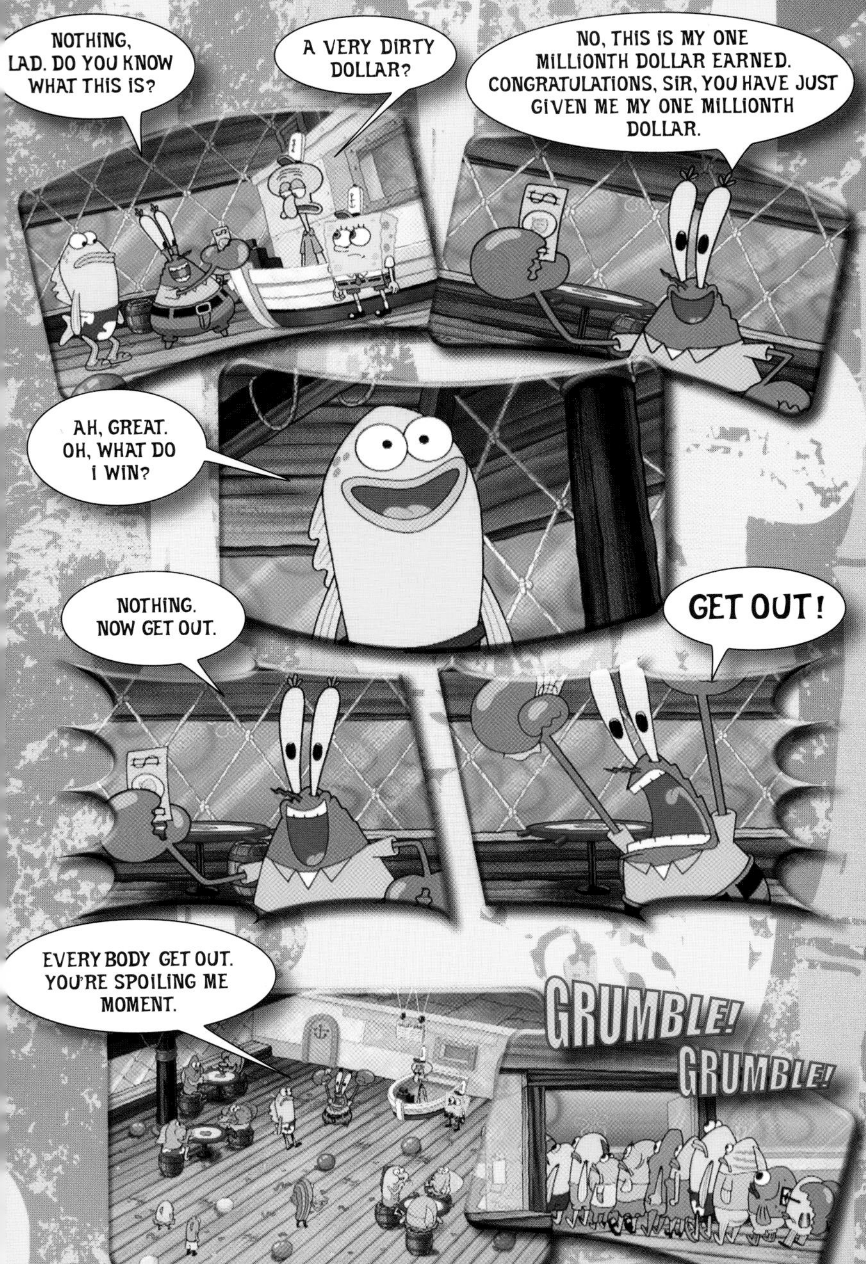
NOTHING, LAD. DO YOU KNOW WHAT THIS IS?
A VERY DIRTY DOLLAR?
NO, THIS IS MY ONE MILLIONTH DOLLAR EARNED. CONGRATULATIONS, SIR, YOU HAVE JUST GIVEN ME MY ONE MILLIONTH DOLLAR.
AH, GREAT. OH, WHAT DO I WIN?
NOTHING. NOW GET OUT.
GET OUT!
EVERY BODY GET OUT. YOU'RE SPOILING ME MOMENT.
GRUMBLE!
GRUMBLE!

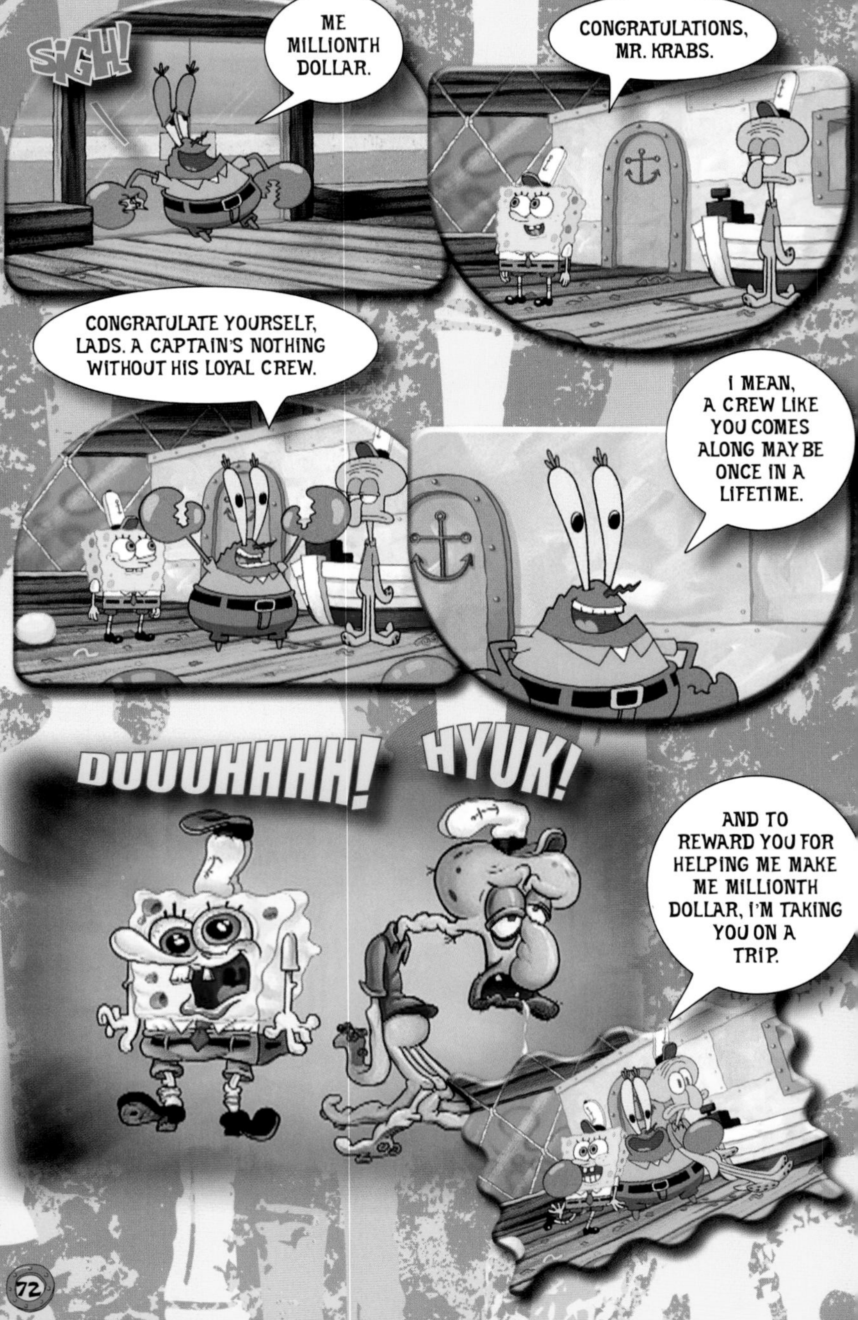
SIGH!
ME MILLIONTH DOLLAR.
CONGRATULATIONS, MR. KRABS.
CONGRATULATE YOURSELF, LADS. A CAPTAIN'S NOTHING WITHOUT HIS LOYAL CREW.
I MEAN, A CREW LIKE YOU COMES ALONG MAYBE ONCE IN A LIFETIME.
DUUUHHHH!
HYUK!
AND TO REWARD YOU FOR HELPING ME MAKE ME MILLIONTH DOLLAR, I'M TAKING YOU ON A TRIP.

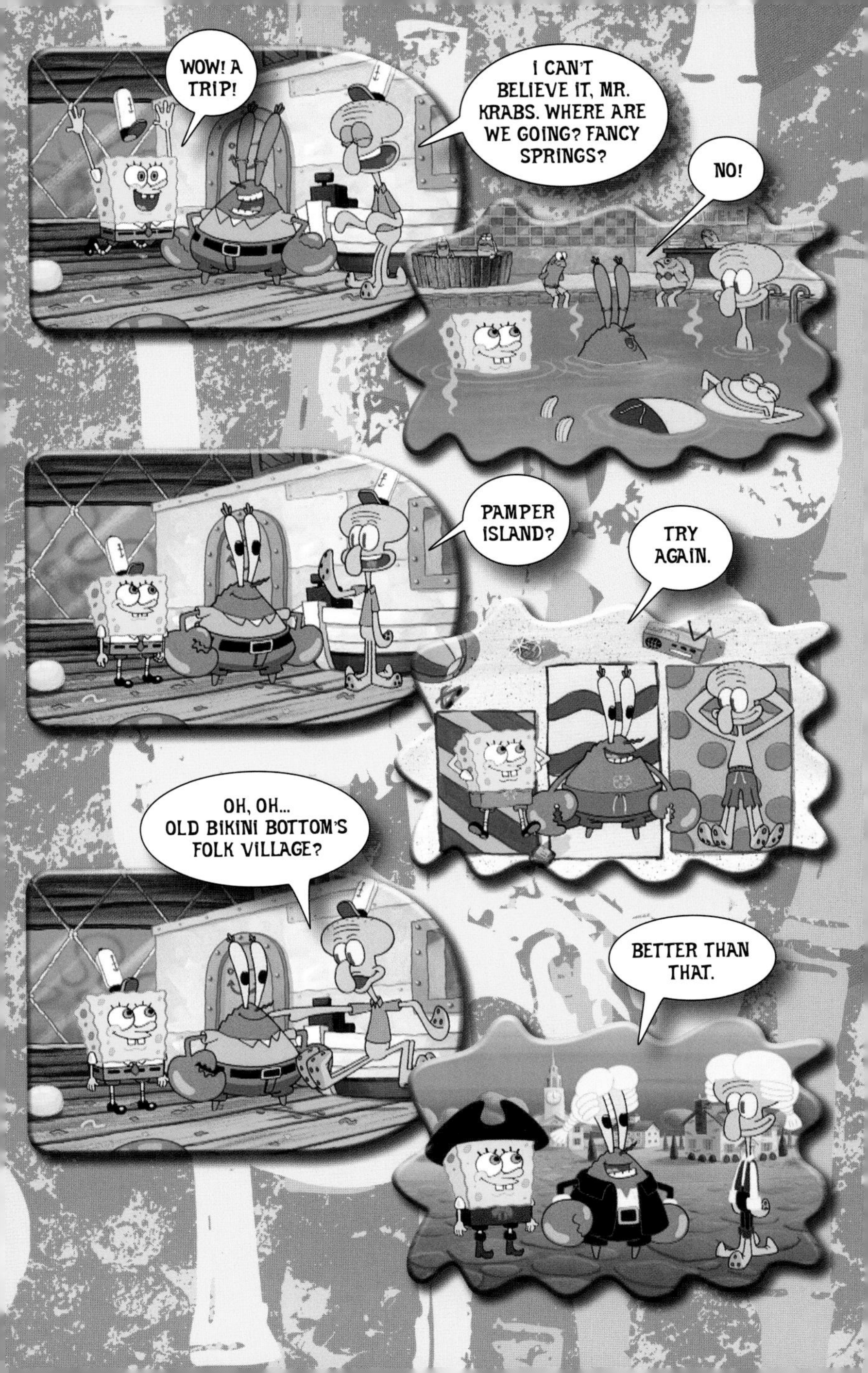
WOW! A TRIP!
I CAN'T BELIEVE IT, MR. KRABS. WHERE ARE WE GOING? FANCY SPRINGS?
NO!
PAMPER ISLAND?
TRY AGAIN.
OH, OH... OLD BIKINI BOTTOM'S FOLK VILLAGE?
BETTER THAN THAT.

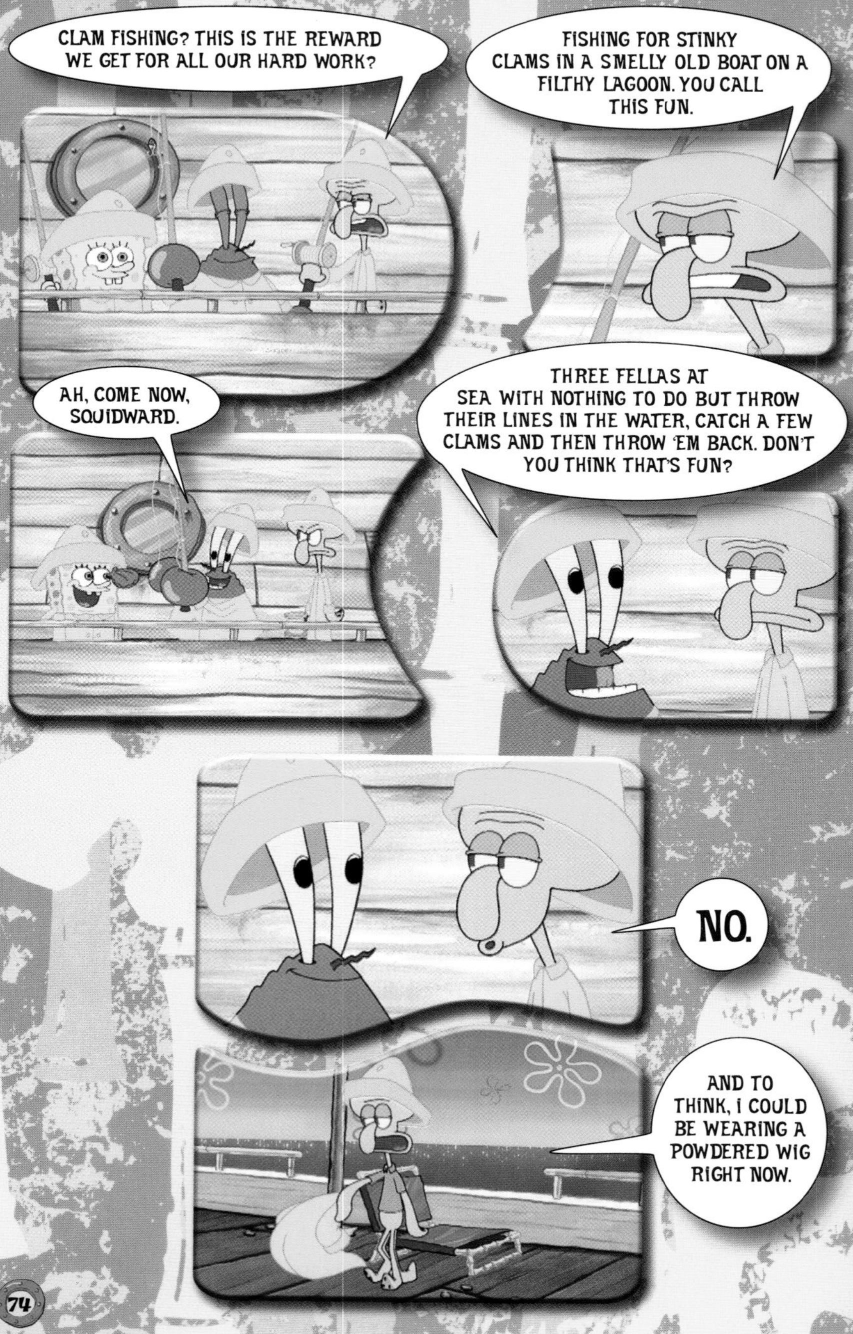
CLAM FISHING? THIS IS THE REWARD WE GET FOR ALL OUR HARD WORK?
FISHING FOR STINKY CLAMS IN A SMELLY OLD BOAT ON A FILTHY LAGOON. YOU CALL THIS FUN.
AH, COME NOW, SQUIDWARD.
THREE FELLAS AT SEA WITH NOTHING TO DO BUT THROW THEIR LINES IN THE WATER, CATCH A FEW CLAMS AND THEN THROW 'EM BACK. DON'T YOU THINK THAT'S FUN?
NO.
AND TO THINK, I COULD BE WEARING A POWDERED WIG RIGHT NOW.

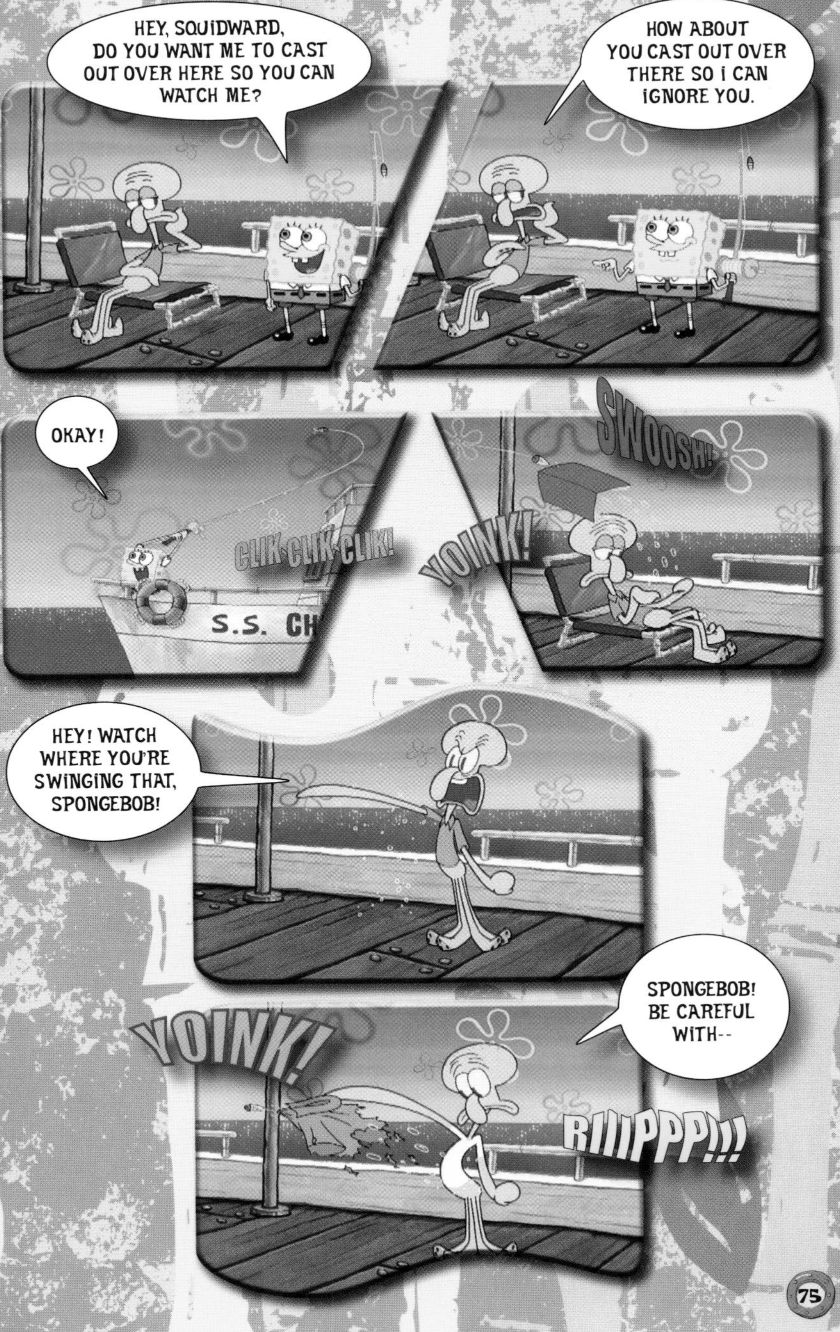
HEY, SQUIDWARD, DO YOU WANT ME TO CAST OUT OVER HERE SO YOU CAN WATCH ME?
HOW ABOUT YOU CAST OUT OVER THERE SO I CAN IGNORE YOU.
OKAY!
CLIK CLIK CLIK!
S.S. CH
SWOOSH!
YOINK!
HEY! WATCH WHERE YOU'RE SWINGING THAT, SPONGEBOB!
YOINK!
SPONGEBOB! BE CAREFUL WITH--
RIIIPPP!!!

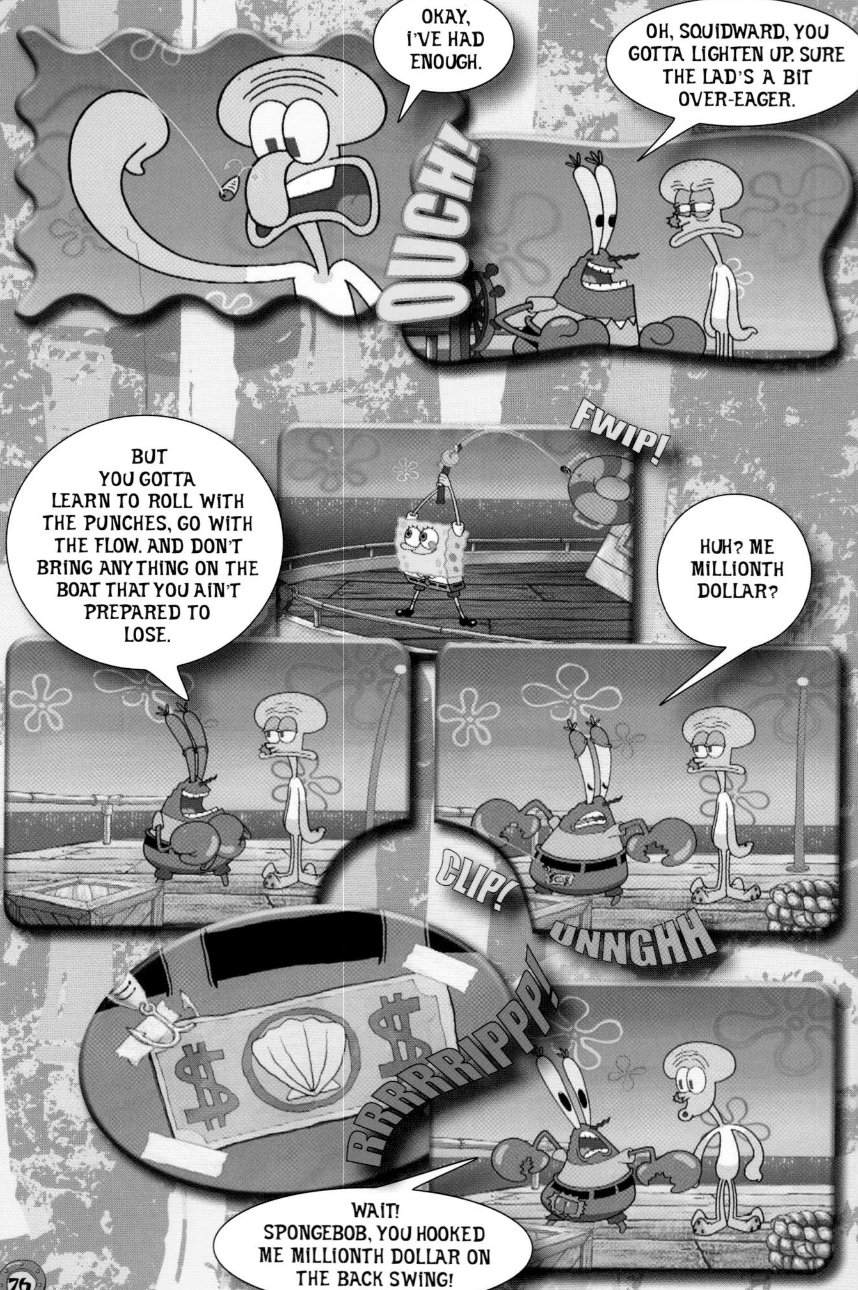
OKAY, I'VE HAD ENOUGH.
OUCH!
OH, SQUIDWARD, YOU GOTTA LIGHTEN UP. SURE THE LAD'S A BIT OVER-EAGER.
FWIP!
BUT YOU GOTTA LEARN TO ROLL WITH THE PUNCHES, GO WITH THE FLOW. AND DON'T BRING ANYTHING ON THE BOAT THAT YOU AIN'T PREPARED TO LOSE.
HUH? ME MILLIONTH DOLLAR?
CLIP!
UNNGHH
RRRRRIPPP!
WAIT! SPONGEBOB, YOU HOOKED ME MILLIONTH DOLLAR ON THE BACK SWING!

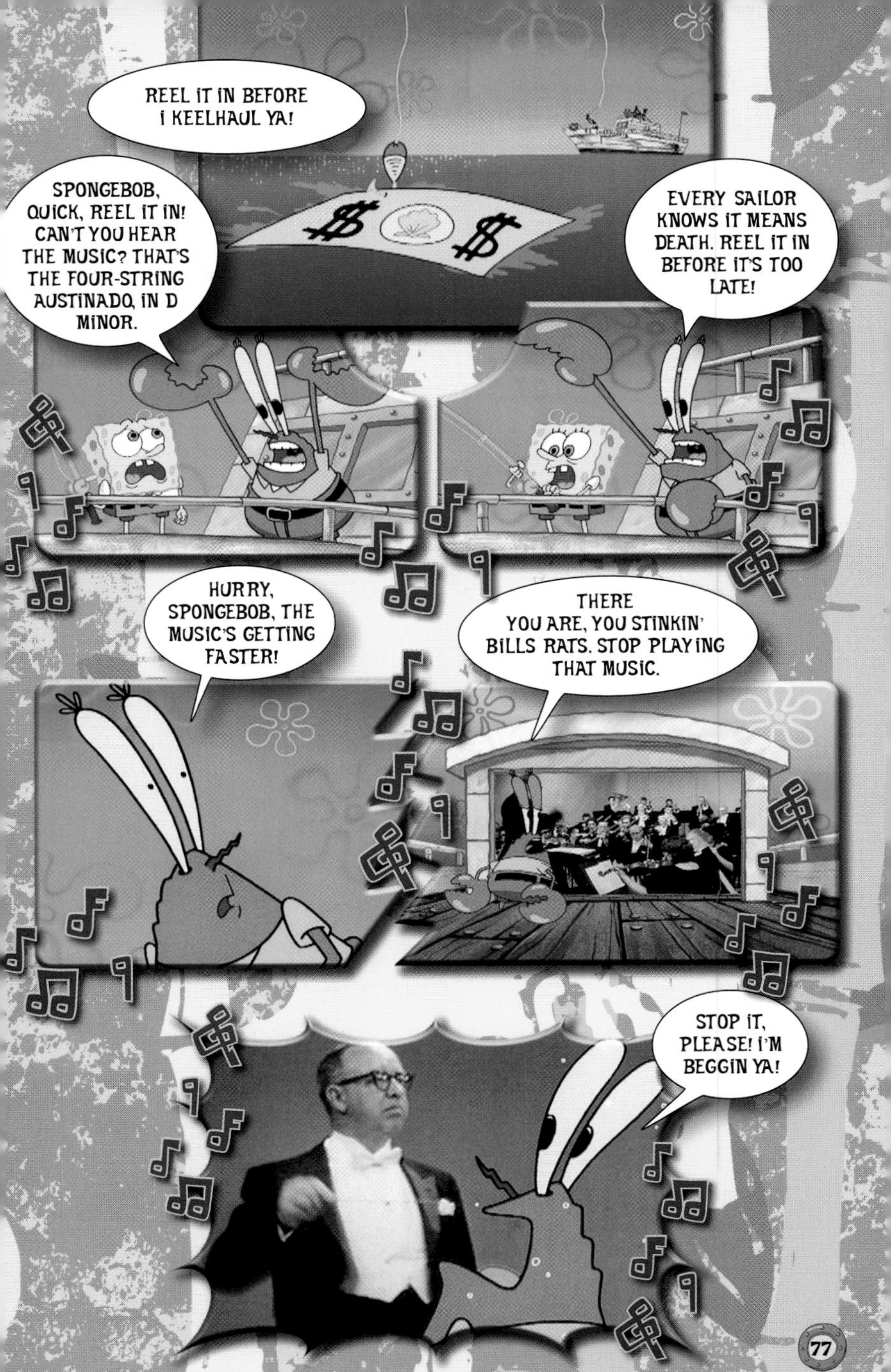
REEL IT IN BEFORE I KEELHAUL YA!
SPONGEBOB, QUICK, REEL IT IN! CAN'T YOU HEAR THE MUSIC? THAT'S THE FOUR-STRING AUSTINADO, IN D MINOR.
EVERY SAILOR KNOWS IT MEANS DEATH. REEL IT IN BEFORE IT'S TOO LATE!
HURRY, SPONGEBOB, THE MUSIC'S GETTING FASTER!
THERE YOU ARE, YOU STINKIN' BILLS RATS. STOP PLAYING THAT MUSIC.
STOP IT, PLEASE! I'M BEGGIN YA!

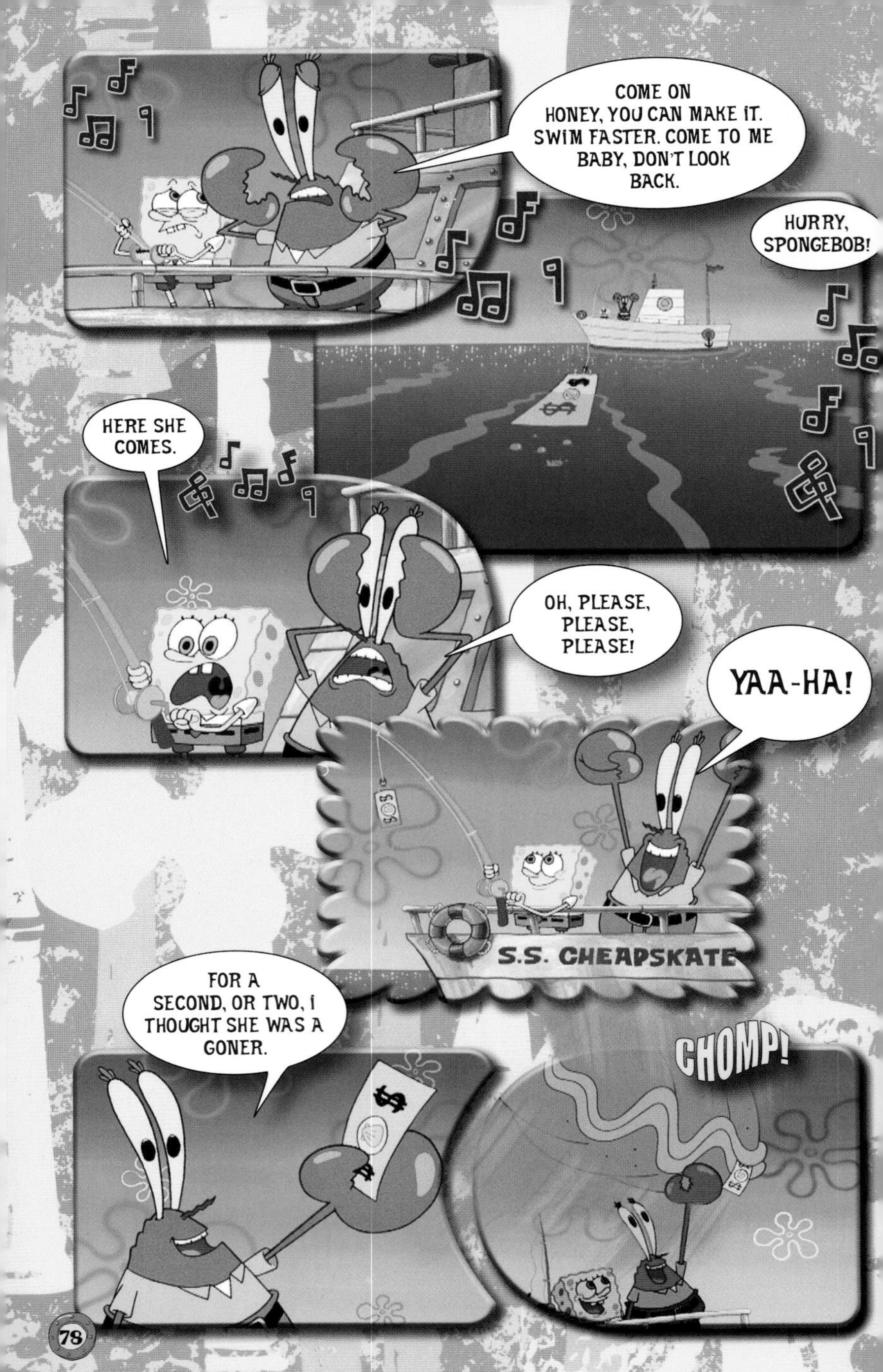
COME ON HONEY, YOU CAN MAKE IT. SWIM FASTER. COME TO ME BABY, DON'T LOOK BACK.
HURRY, SPONGEBOB!
HERE SHE COMES.
OH, PLEASE, PLEASE, PLEASE!
YAA-HA!
S.S. CHEAPSKATE
FOR A SECOND, OR TWO, I THOUGHT SHE WAS A GONER.
CHOMP!

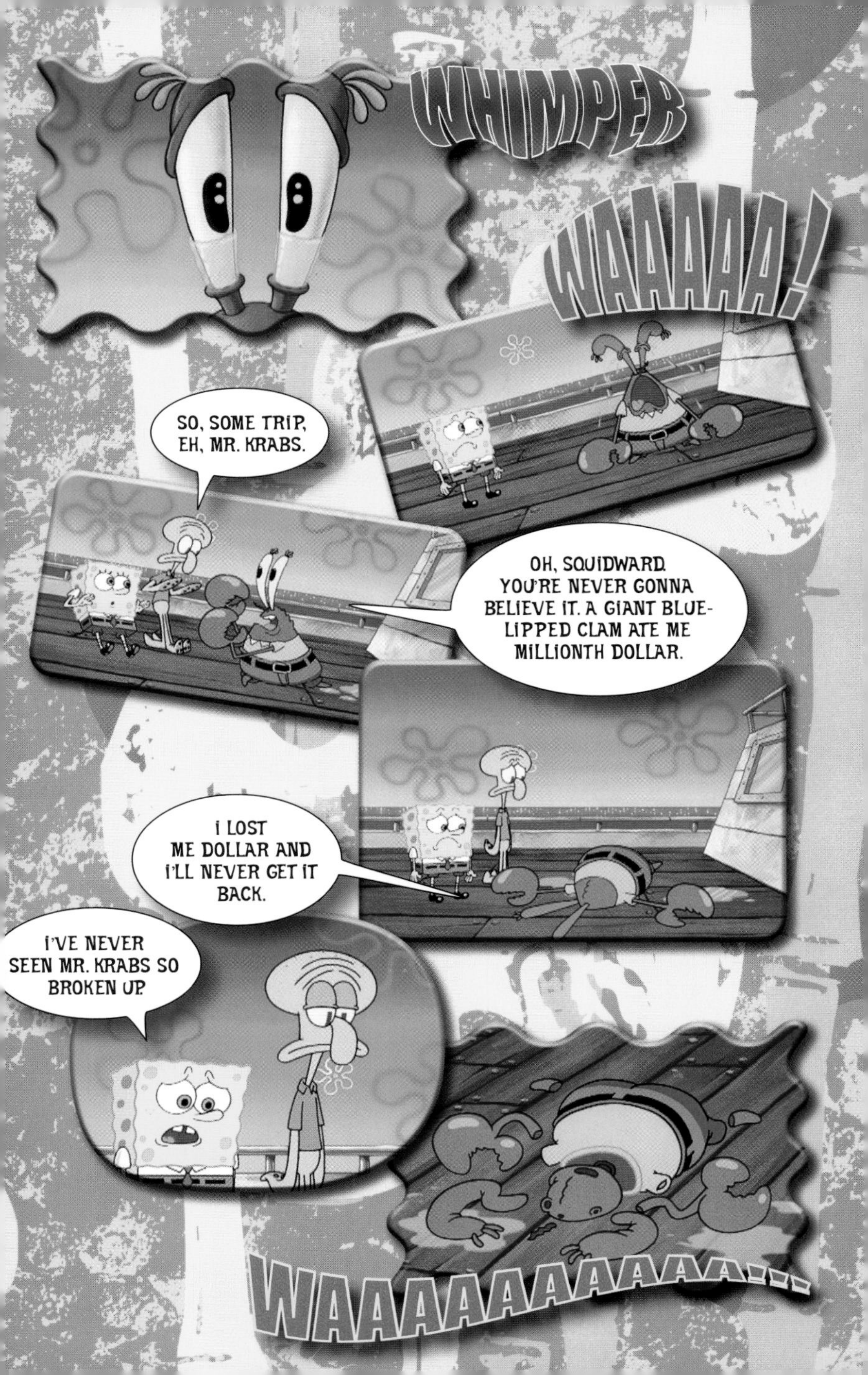
WHIMPER
WAAAAAA!
SO, SOME TRIP, EH, MR. KRABS.
OH, SQUIDWARD. YOU'RE NEVER GONNA BELIEVE IT. A GIANT BLUE-LIPPED CLAM ATE ME MILLIONTH DOLLAR.
I LOST ME DOLLAR AND I'LL NEVER GET IT BACK.
I'VE NEVER SEEN MR. KRABS SO BROKEN UP.
WAAAAAAAAAAA...

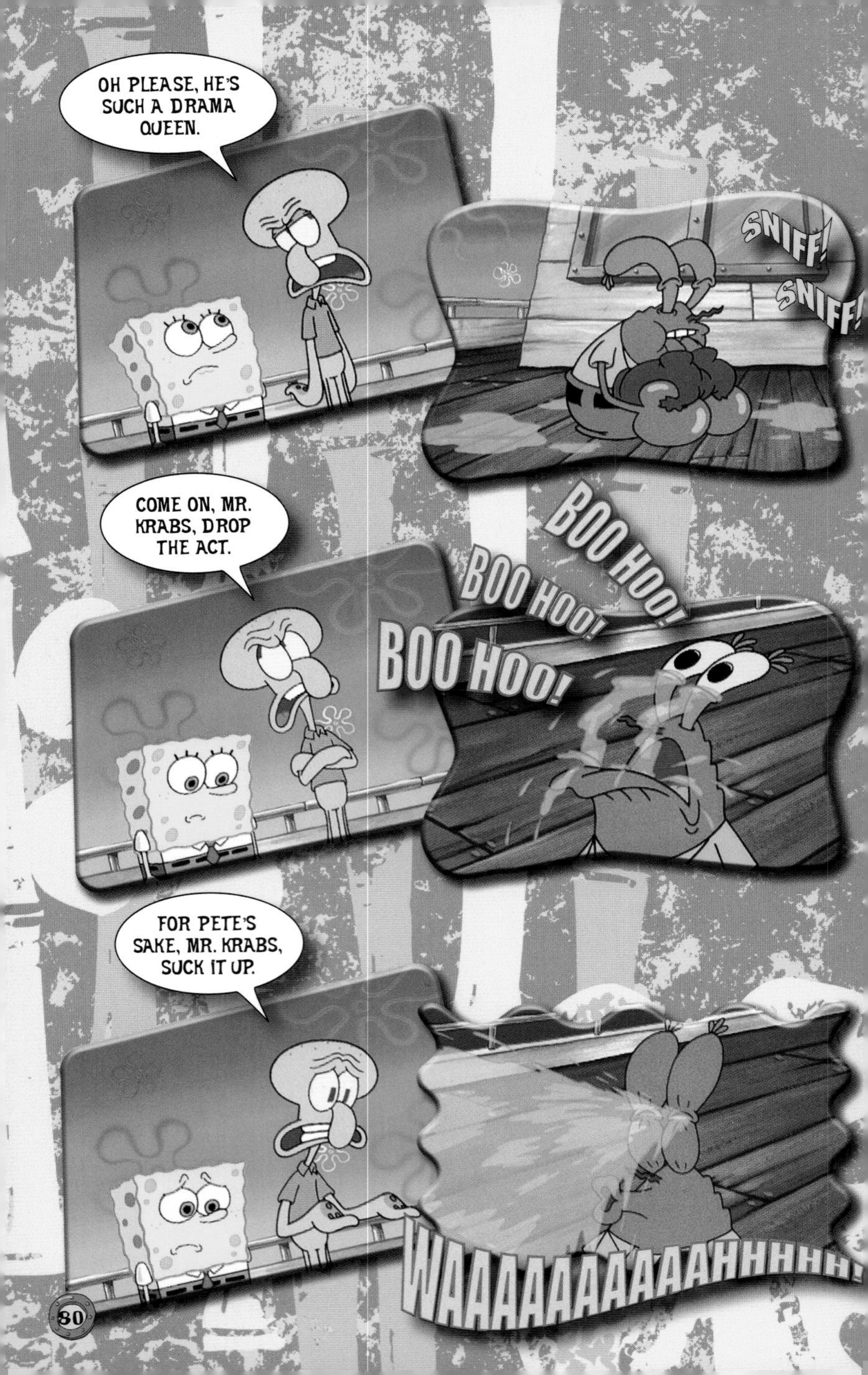
OH PLEASE, HE'S SUCH A DRAMA QUEEN.
SNIFF!
SNIFF!
COME ON, MR. KRABS, DROP THE ACT.
BOO HOO!
BOO HOO!
BOO HOO!
FOR PETE'S SAKE, MR. KRABS, SUCK IT UP.
WAAAAAAAAAAHHHHH!

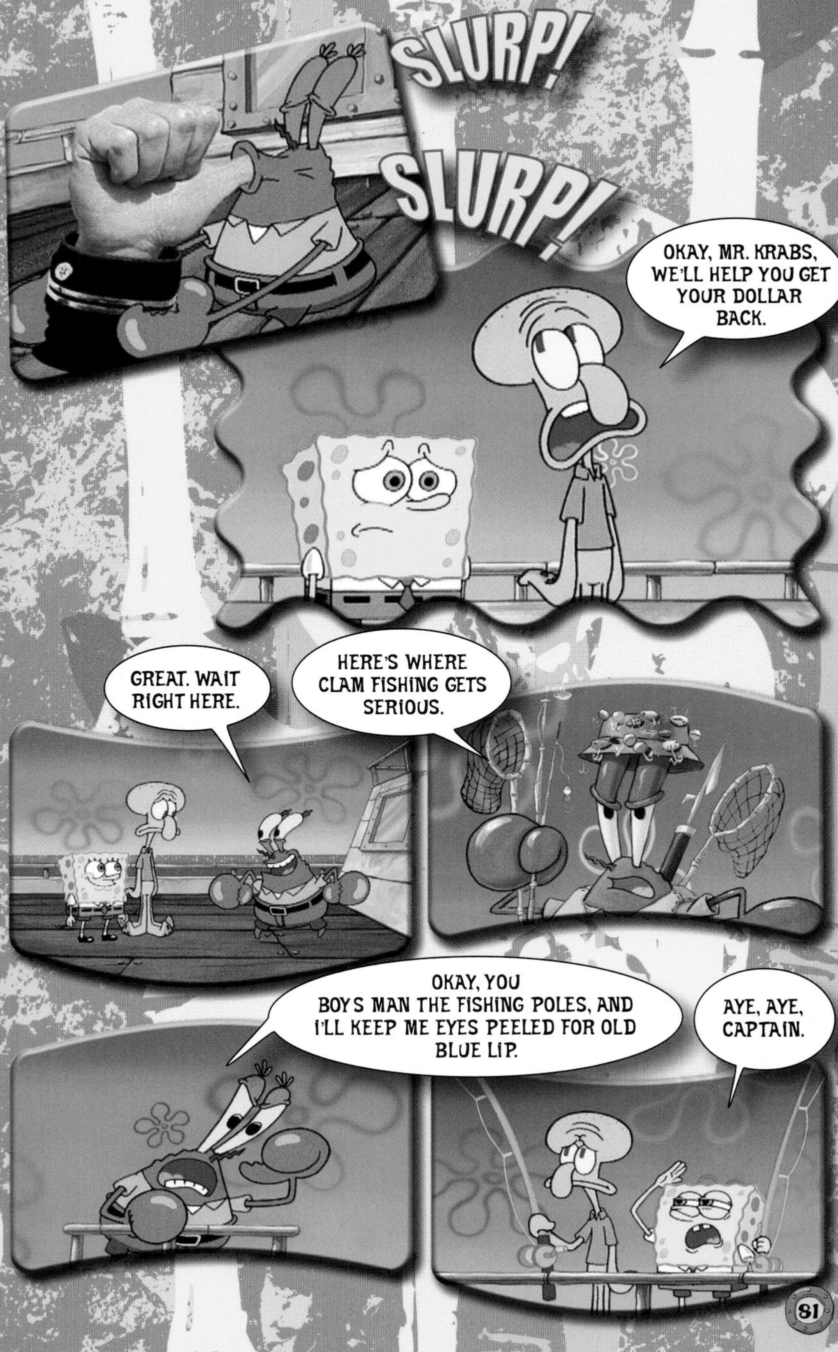
SLURP!
SLURP!
OKAY, MR. KRABS, WE'LL HELP YOU GET YOUR DOLLAR BACK.
GREAT. WAIT RIGHT HERE.
HERE'S WHERE CLAM FISHING GETS SERIOUS.
OKAY, YOU BOYS MAN THE FISHING POLES, AND I'LL KEEP ME EYES PEELED FOR OLD BLUE LIP.
AYE, AYE, CAPTAIN.

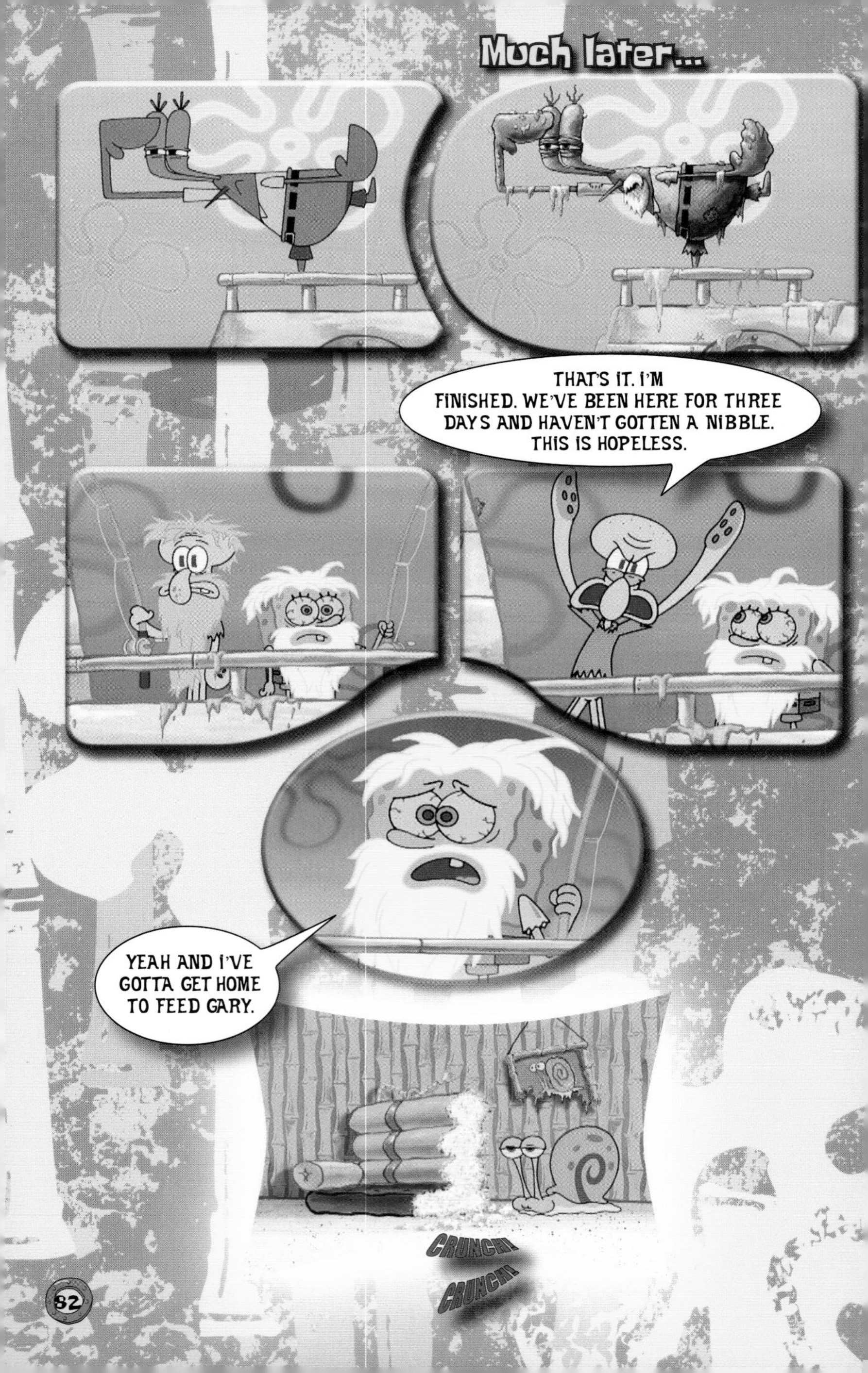
Much later...
THAT'S IT. I'M FINISHED. WE'VE BEEN HERE FOR THREE DAYS AND HAVEN'T GOTTEN A NIBBLE. THIS IS HOPELESS.
YEAH AND I'VE GOTTA GET HOME TO FEED GARY.
CRUNCH!
CRUNCH!

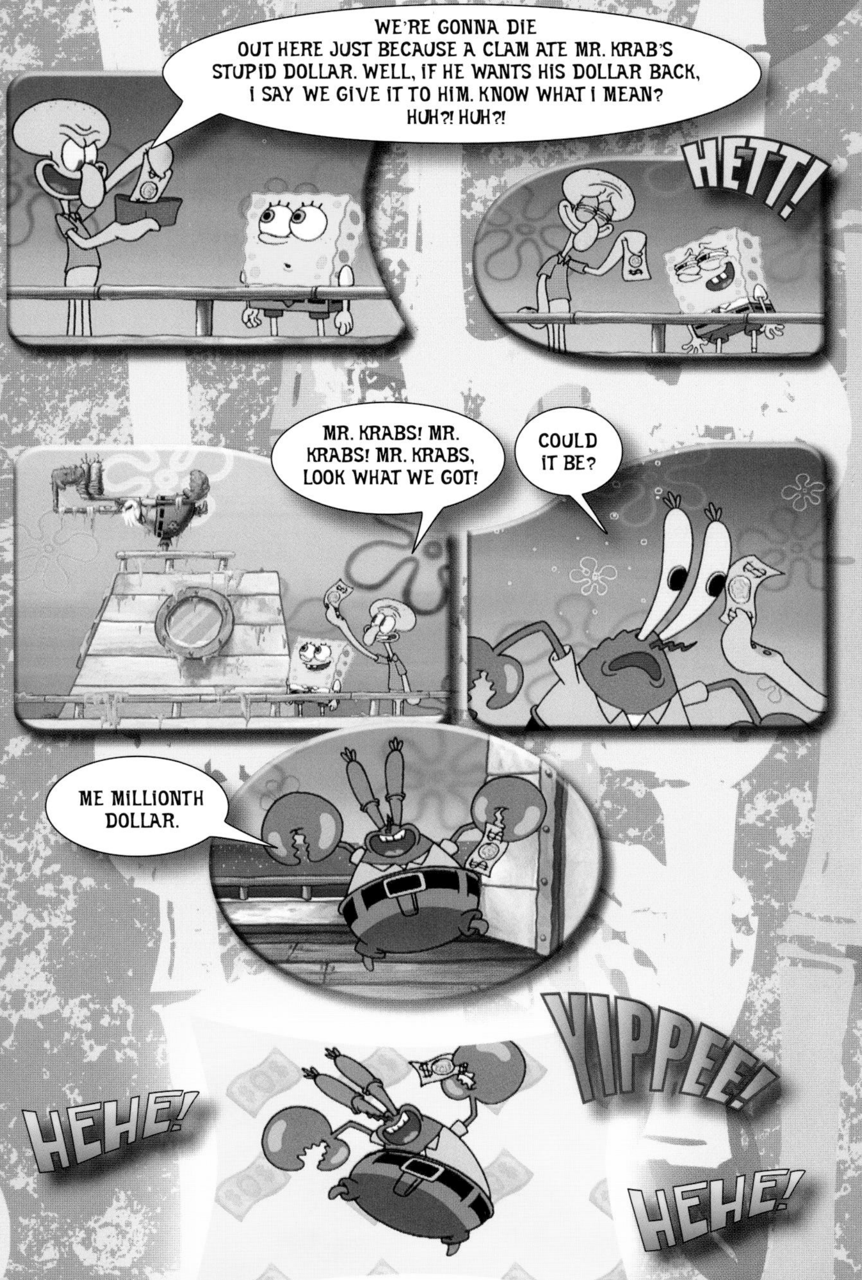
WE'RE GONNA DIE OUT HERE JUST BECAUSE A CLAM ATE MR. KRAB'S STUPID DOLLAR. WELL, IF HE WANTS HIS DOLLAR BACK, I SAY WE GIVE IT TO HIM. KNOW WHAT I MEAN? HUH?! HUH?!
HETT!
MR. KRABS! MR. KRABS! MR. KRABS, LOOK WHAT WE GOT!
COULD IT BE?
ME MILLIONTH DOLLAR.
YIPPEE!
HEHE!
HEHE!

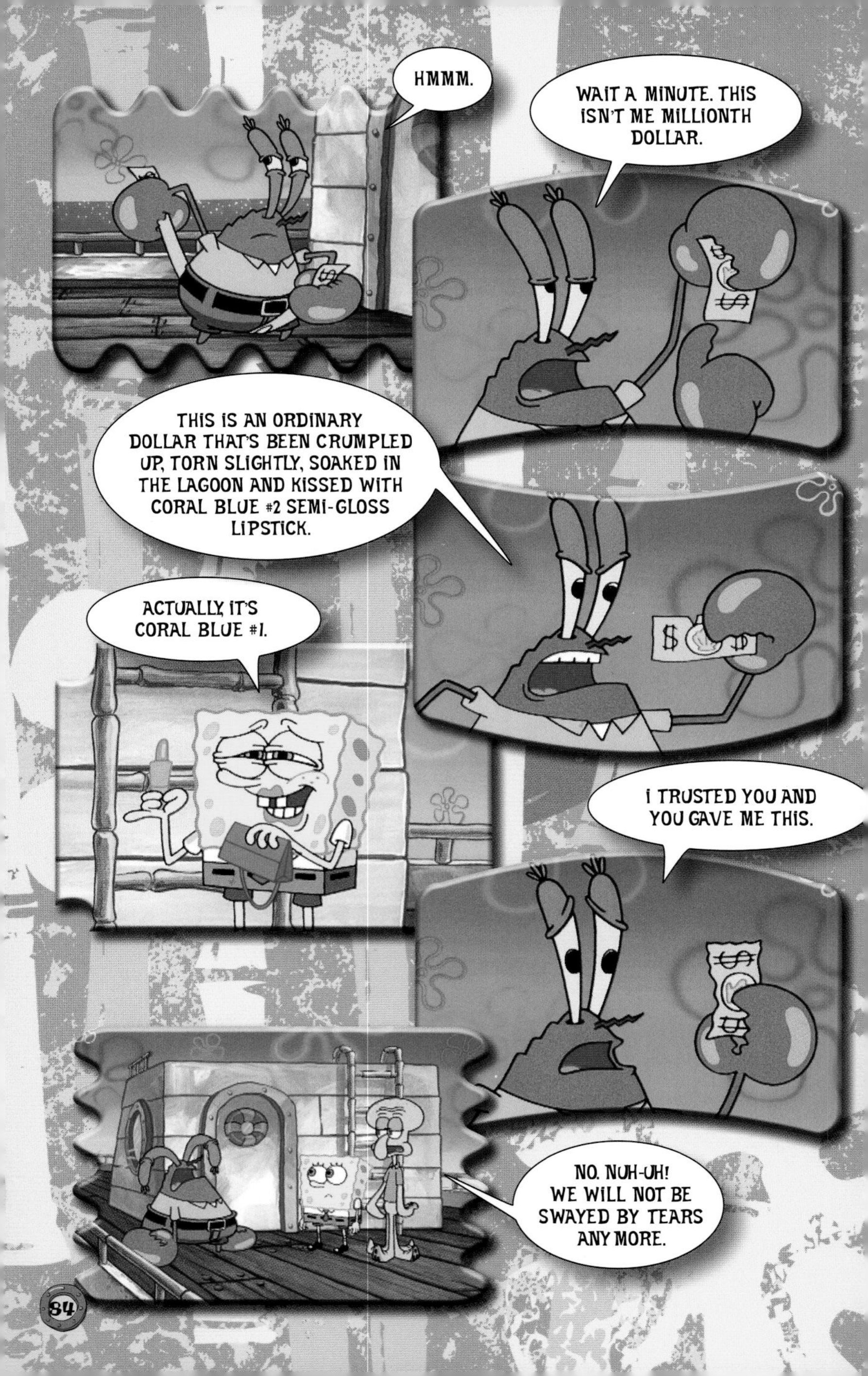

HMMM.
WAIT A MINUTE. THIS ISN'T ME MILLIONTH DOLLAR.
THIS IS AN ORDINARY DOLLAR THAT'S BEEN CRUMPLED UP, TORN SLIGHTLY, SOAKED IN THE LAGOON AND KISSED WITH CORAL BLUE #2 SEMI-GLOSS LIPSTICK.
ACTUALLY, IT'S CORAL BLUE #1.
I TRUSTED YOU AND YOU GAVE ME THIS.
NO. NUH-UH! WE WILL NOT BE SWAYED BY TEARS ANY MORE.

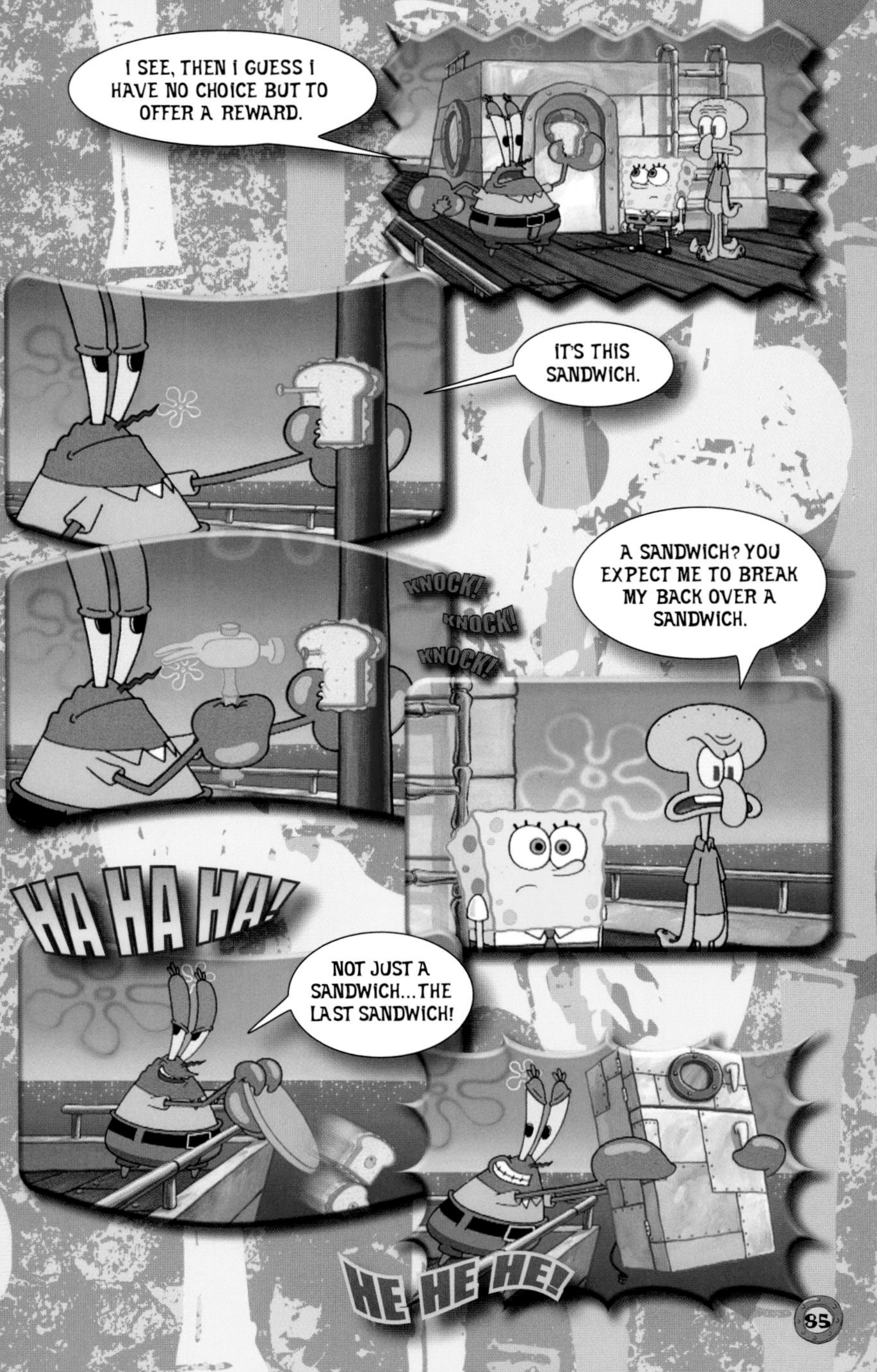

I SEE, THEN I GUESS I HAVE NO CHOICE BUT TO OFFER A REWARD.
IT'S THIS SANDWICH.
KNOCK! KNOCK! KNOCK!
A SANDWICH? YOU EXPECT ME TO BREAK MY BACK OVER A SANDWICH.
HA HA HA!
NOT JUST A SANDWICH...THE LAST SANDWICH!
HE HE HE!

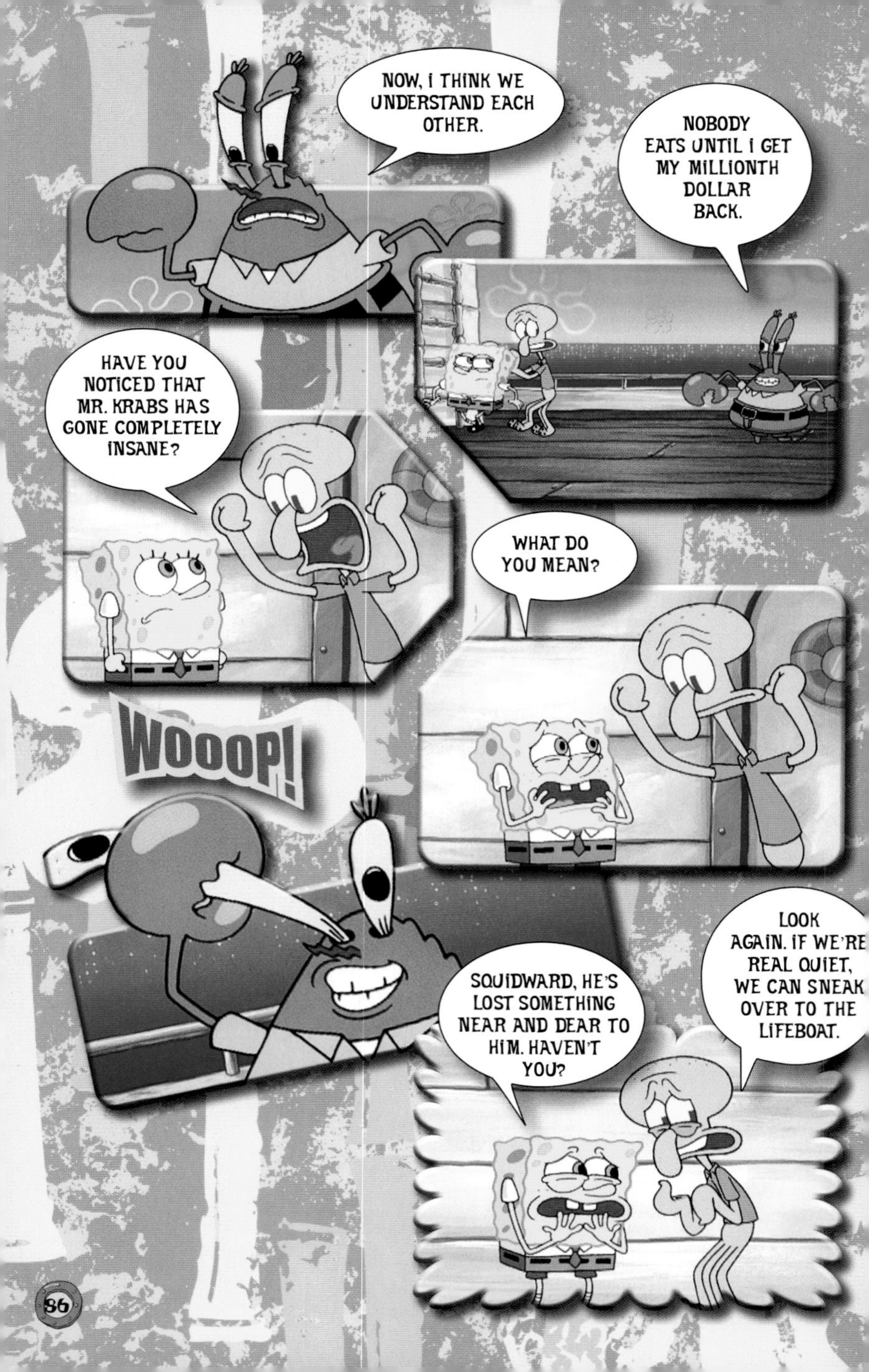
NOW, I THINK WE UNDERSTAND EACH OTHER.
NOBODY EATS UNTIL I GET MY MILLIONTH DOLLAR BACK.
HAVE YOU NOTICED THAT MR. KRABS HAS GONE COMPLETELY INSANE?
WHAT DO YOU MEAN?
WOOOP!
SQUIDWARD, HE'S LOST SOMETHING NEAR AND DEAR TO HIM. HAVEN'T YOU?
LOOK AGAIN. IF WE'RE REAL QUIET, WE CAN SNEAK OVER TO THE LIFEBOAT.

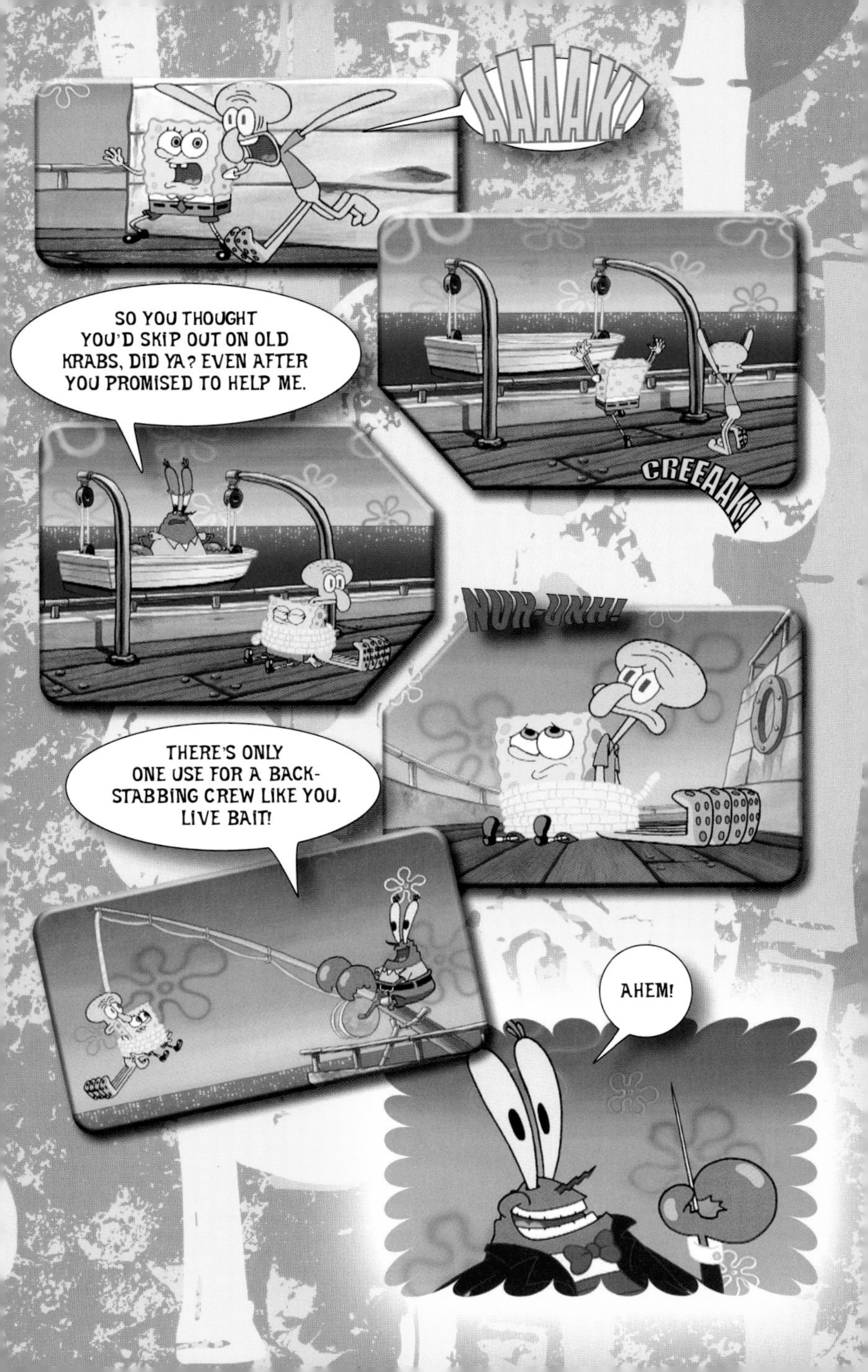
AAAAK!
SO YOU THOUGHT YOU'D SKIP OUT ON OLD KRABS, DID YA? EVEN AFTER YOU PROMISED TO HELP ME.
CREEAAK!
NUH-UNH!
THERE'S ONLY ONE USE FOR A BACK-STABBING CREW LIKE YOU. LIVE BAIT!
AHEM!

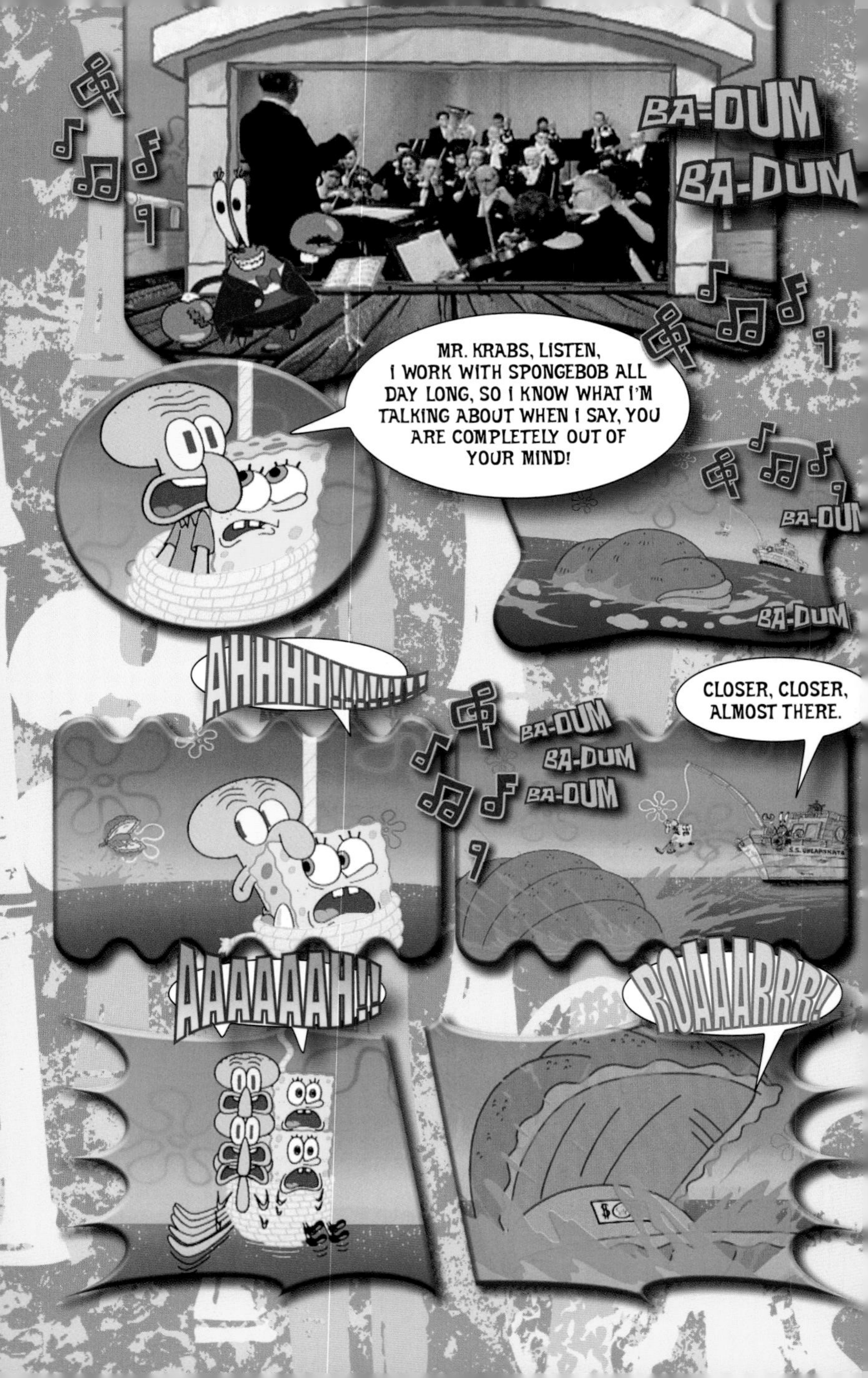
BA-DUM
BA-DUM
MR. KRABS, LISTEN, I WORK WITH SPONGEBOB ALL DAY LONG, SO I KNOW WHAT I'M TALKING ABOUT WHEN I SAY, YOU ARE COMPLETELY OUT OF YOUR MIND!
BA-DUM
AHHHH!!!!!!!
BA-DUM
BA-DUM
BA-DUM
CLOSER, CLOSER, ALMOST THERE.
AAAAAAH!!!
ROAAARRR!

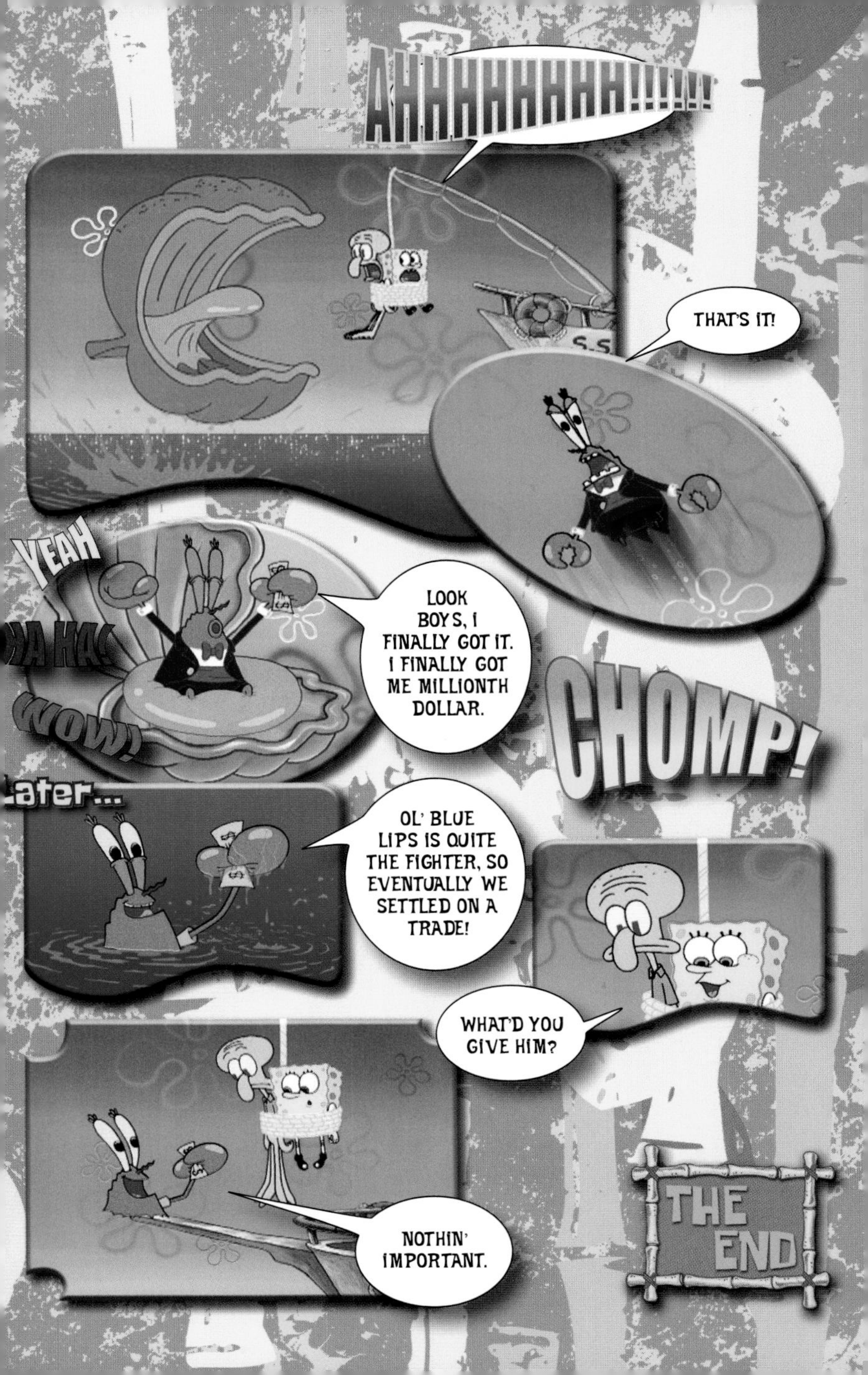
AHHHHHHHH!!!!!!
THAT'S IT!
YEAH
HA HA!
WOW!
LOOK BOYS, I FINALLY GOT IT. I FINALLY GOT ME MILLIONTH DOLLAR.
CHOMP!
Later...
OL' BLUE LIPS IS QUITE THE FIGHTER, SO EVENTUALLY WE SETTLED ON A TRADE!
WHAT'D YOU GIVE HIM?
NOTHIN' IMPORTANT.
THE END

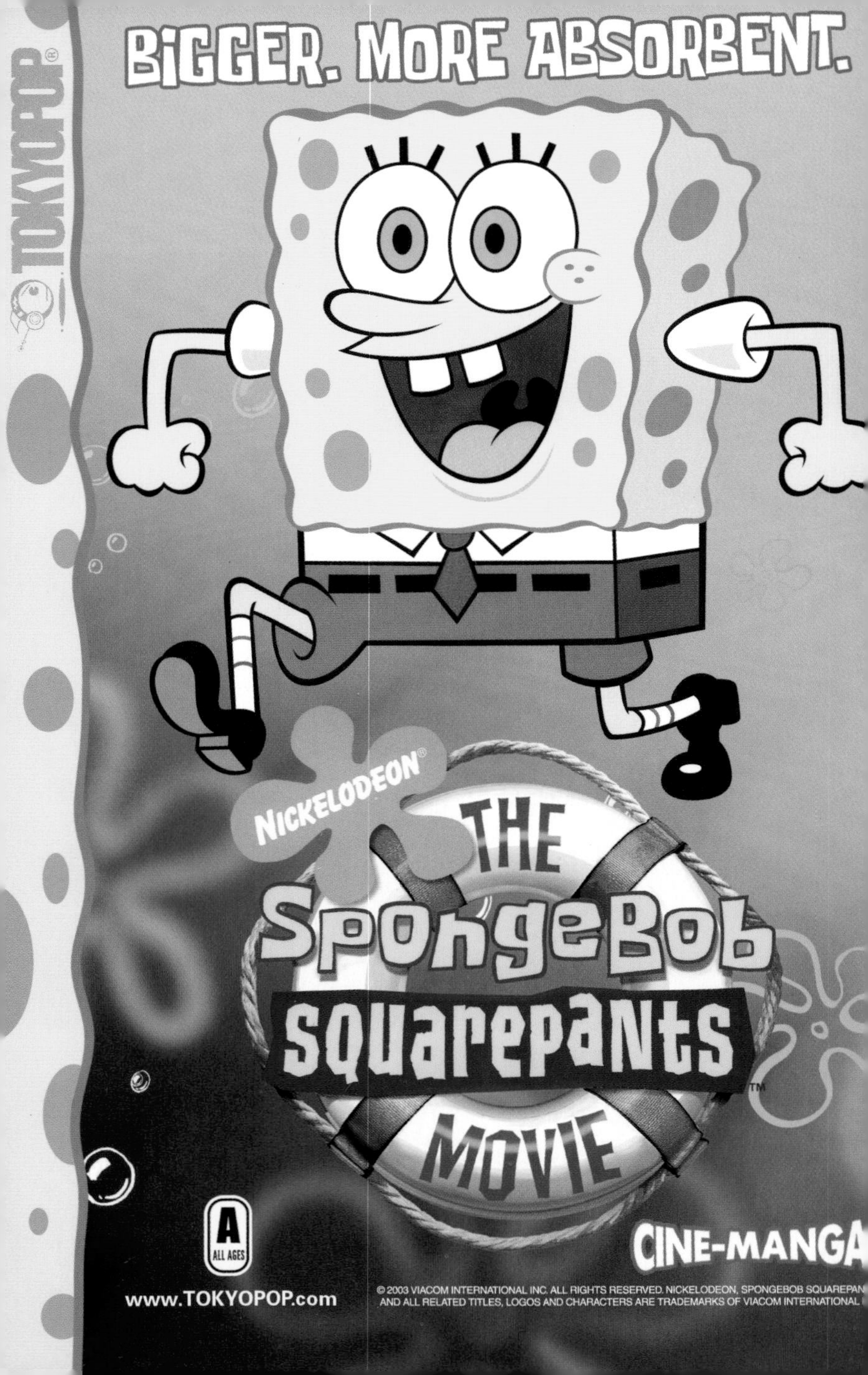
TOKYOPOP®
BIGGER. MORE ABSORBENT.
NICKELODEON®
THE SpongeBob SquarePants MOVIE™
A ALL AGES
CINE-MANGA
www.TOKYOPOP.com
© 2003 VIACOM INTERNATIONAL INC. ALL RIGHTS RESERVED. NICKELODEON, SPONGEBOB SQUAREPAN
AND ALL RELATED TITLES, LOGOS AND CHARACTERS ARE TRADEMARKS OF VIACOM INTERNATIONAL

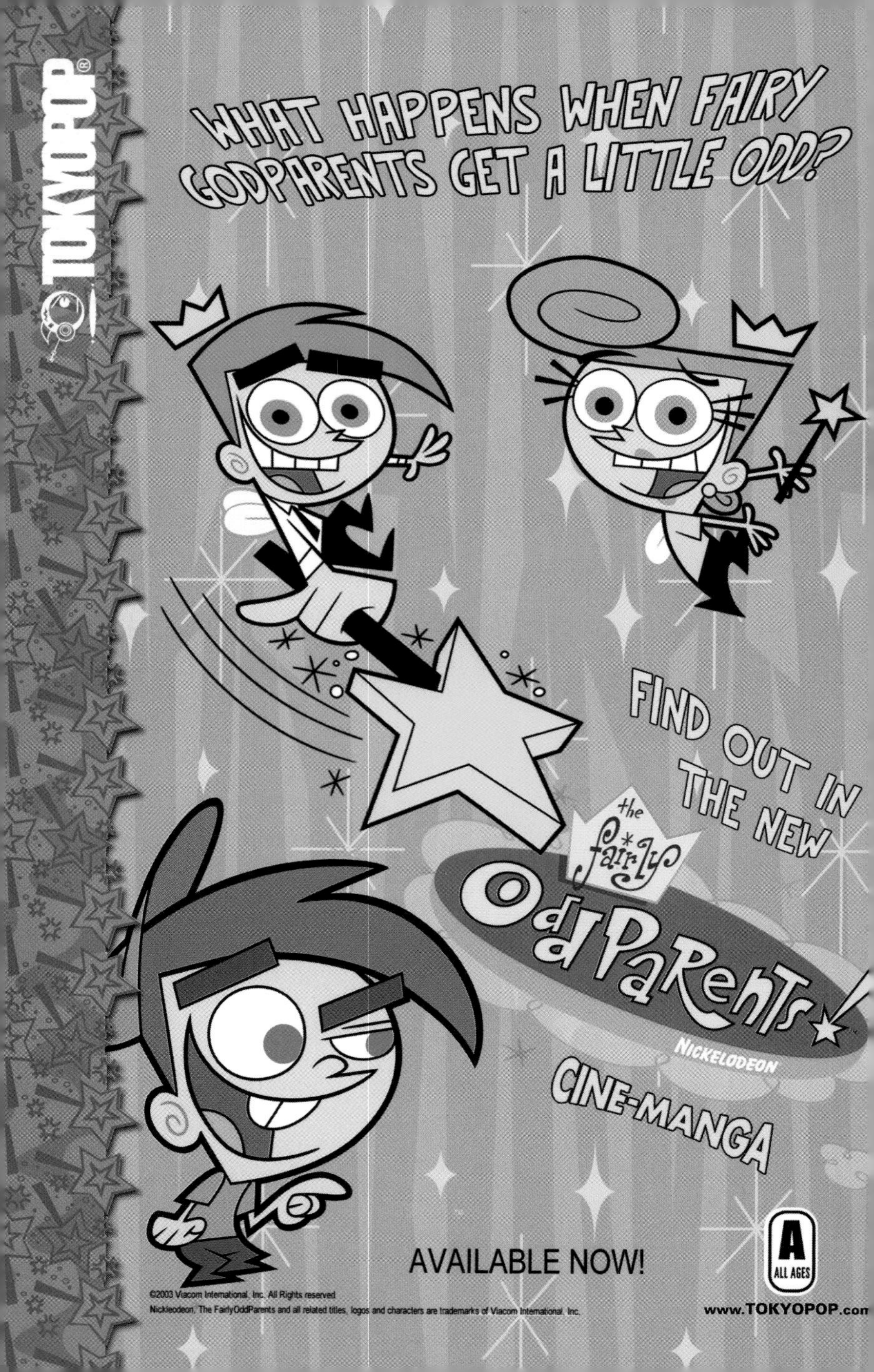
TOKYOPOP®
WHAT HAPPENS WHEN FAIRY GODPARENTS GET A LITTLE ODD?
FIND OUT IN THE NEW
the fairly OddParents!
NICKELODEON
CINE-MANGA
AVAILABLE NOW!
A
ALL AGES
©2003 Viacom International, Inc. All Rights reserved
Nickleodeon, The FairlyOddParents and all related titles, logos and characters are trademarks of Viacom International, Inc.
www.TOKYOPOP.com

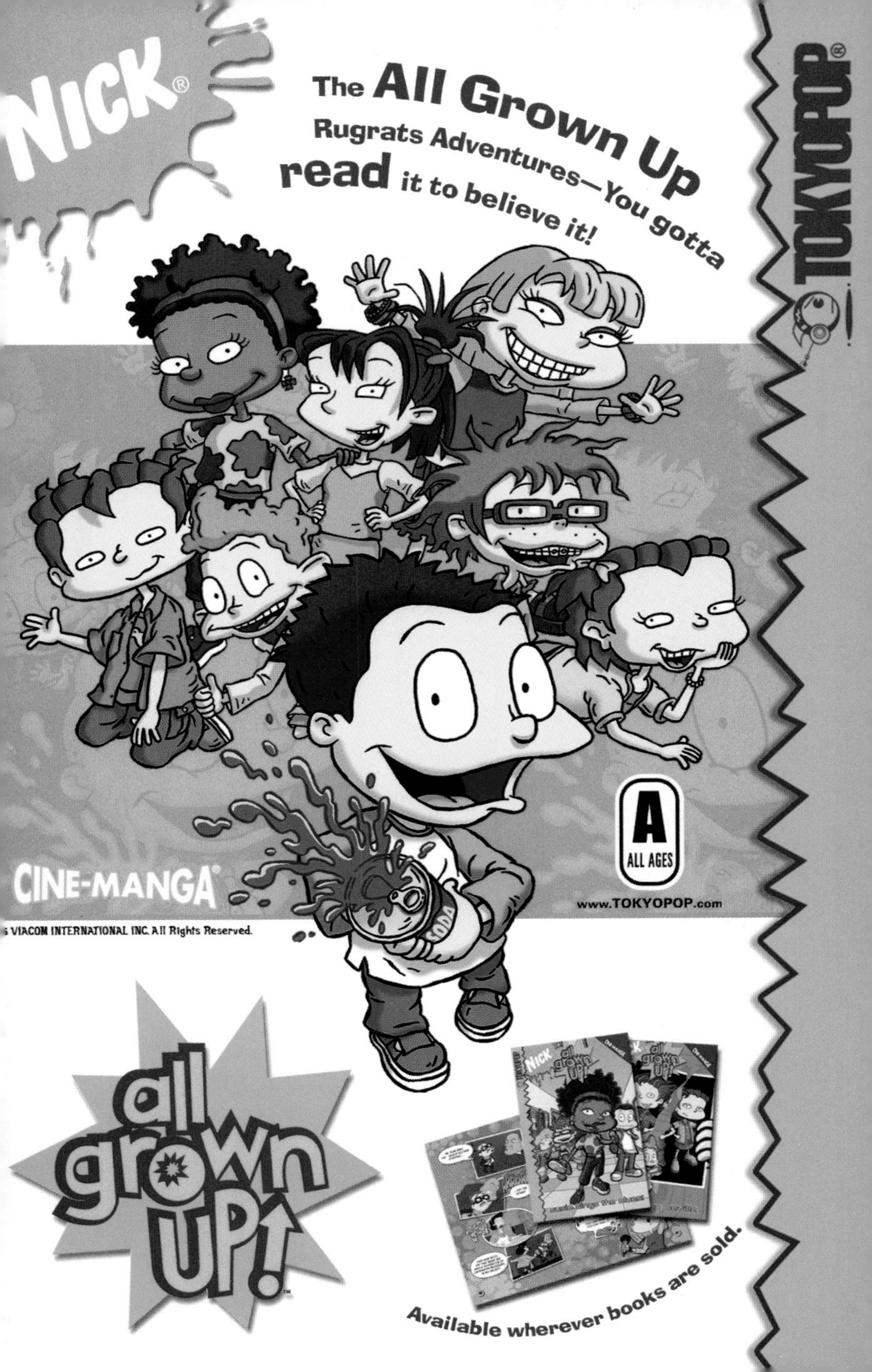
NICK
TOKYOPOP
The All Grown Up
Rugrats Adventures—You gotta
read it to believe it!
A
ALL AGES
CINE-MANGA
www.TOKYOPOP.com
VIACOM INTERNATIONAL INC. All Rights Reserved.
SODA
all grown up!
Available wherever books are sold.

ALSO AVAILABLE FROM TOKYOPOP®

MANGA

.HACK//LEGEND OF THE TWILIGHT
ALICHINO
ANGELIC LAYER
BABY BIRTH
BRAIN POWERED
BRIGADOON
B'TX
CANDIDATE FOR GODDESS, THE
CARDCAPTOR SAKURA
CARDCAPTOR SAKURA - MASTER OF THE CLOW
CHRONICLES OF THE CURSED SWORD
CLAMP SCHOOL DETECTIVES
CLOVER
COMIC PARTY
CORRECTOR YUI
COWBOY BEBOP
COWBOY BEBOP: SHOOTING STAR
CRESCENT MOON
CROSS
CULDCEPT
CYBORG 009
D•N•ANGEL
DEARS
DEMON DIARY
DEMON OROR0N, THE
DIGIMON
DIGIMON TAMERS
DIGIMON ZERO TWO
DRAGON HUNTER
DRAGON KNIGHTS
DRAGON VOICE
DREAM SAGA
DUKLYON: CLAMP SCHOOL DEFENDERS
ET CETERA
ETERNITY
FAERIES' LANDING
FLCL
FLOWER OF THE DEEP SLEEP
FORBIDDEN DANCE
FRUITS BASKET
G GUNDAM
GATEKEEPERS
GIRL GOT GAME
GUNDAM SEED ASTRAY
GUNDAM SEED ASTRAY R
GUNDAM WING
GUNDAM WING: BATTLEFIELD OF PACIFISTS
GUNDAM WING: ENDLESS WALTZ
GUNDAM WING: THE LAST OUTPOST (G-UNIT)
HANDS OFF!

HARLEM BEAT
HYPER RUNE
I.N.V.U.
INITIAL D
INSTANT TEEN: JUST ADD NUTS
JING: KING OF BANDITS
JING: KING OF BANDITS - TWILIGHT TALES
JULINE
KARE KANO
KILL ME, KISS ME
KINDAICHI CASE FILES, THE
KING OF HELL
KODOCHA: SANA'S STAGE
LAGOON ENGINE
LEGEND OF CHUN HYANG, THE
LILING-PO
LOVE OR MONEY
MAGIC KNIGHT RAYEARTH I
MAGIC KNIGHT RAYEARTH II
MAN OF MANY FACES
MARMALADE BOY
MARS
MARS: HORSE WITH NO NAME
MINK
MIRACLE GIRLS
MODEL
MOURYOU KIDEN: LEGEND OF THE NYMPH
NECK AND NECK
ONE
ONE I LOVE, THE
PEACH FUZZ
PEACH GIRL
PEACH GIRL: CHANGE OF HEART
PHD: PHANTASY DEGREE
PITA-TEN
PLANET BLOOD
PLANET LADDER
PLANETES
PRESIDENT DAD
PRINCESS AI
PSYCHIC ACADEMY
QUEEN'S KNIGHT, THE
RAGNAROK
RAVE MASTER
REALITY CHECK
REBIRTH
REBOUND
RISING STARS OF MANGA™,THE
SAILOR MOON
SAINT TAIL
SAMURAI GIRL™ REAL BOUT HIGH SCHOOL

10.19.0

ALSO AVAILABLE FROM  TOKYOPOP®

10.19.04Y